For Mr. Trust

Päivi Nuora

Clover In the Wind

Incredible journey to parenthood

True Story

© 2022 Päivi Nuora

Publisher: BoD – Books on Demand, Helsinki, Finland
Manufacturer: BoD – Books on Demand, Norderstedt, Germany
Translator: Tanja Partanen

ISBN: 978-952-80-6927-0

Contents

OPENING OF THE DIARY 7

EVERYTHING BEGINS WITH BLOOD.. 9

US TWO.. 13

    HOPES AND DREAMS.. 13
    SUN AND FIRE 17
    BREAKDOWN 20

I.. 25

    RACE... 26
    13 LINES AND DROPS 28
    TRY THE TRUTH 38
    FROM DITCH TO FLIGHT 40
    EXPECTED MOMENT 49
    AS A MOTHER IN NEW CULTURE 56

II... 63

    A TICKET TO AFRICA 64
    THROUGH THE STORM 75
    ADAPTION 81
    MR. TRUST... 91
    AFRICAN FAIRY 95
    TOURISMS AND TRIPS 105
    LIFE ON THE FILM TAPE 113
    AT THE BOARDER 124
    MURDER 128

III.. 133

    CLOVER.. 133
    DIAMOND 139

CARDIAC AMBULANCE 149

HOSPITAL CLOWN 155

ONLY STRAIGHT LINE 159

LUCK AND ACCIDENT 159

FORWARD 167

METALBED 172

IV 175

THE SECRET DECISION 175

GOLDEN RING 180

IN THE EYE OF THE STORM 183

DISAPPEARED FATHER 188

TEARS OF HAPPINESS IN DISTANCE 195

THE END 207

OVER THE BOARDER 207

GOOD, THANK YOU 214

EPILOGUE 219

THANK YOU 223

REFERENCE 224

OPENING OF THE DIARY

If you ask what kind of story I am going to tell, I urge you to imagine your greatest hopes and worst fears in the same package so that your hopes are beyond your reach, and you cannot control the course of events. Also, at the same time, you must hide everything from your loved ones. This is what happened in its entirety.

Every day is lived to the fullest and memories of them are reminiscent at the edge of the calendar, photographs, in the rooms of our home, belongings, pending repairs, watered clothes from all the tears of happiness and grief, and torn incisions in the heart. I will tell you how, me and my husband are ready to do anything to acquire that all-peaceful and normal life, that many aspire to have with everyday hobbies and happy experiences. We risk our health, safety and lives to achieve our goals.

On the first visit, one therapist tried to make a mind map to outline my situation. Tried but failed. I realized at the time that writing my story and going through things with my husband is the best way for me to process on everything that has happened. Questions we get from loved ones and their desire to understand everything that happened also encourage me further to tell and write. We have lived a secret life: everything that happened is too deep in us to be able to share on Facebook and too heavy and painful to be even structured in a diary in the middle of events. As I have written our story, I have noticed that sometimes the most complicated path has been just the right one.

The book tells you about an ordinary couple from Finland and their desire to start a family. Our lives are anything but an ordinary story. People's reactions have been amazed and shocked when I have told even the smallest piece of our lives and travels. Listeners wonder how so much could have happened to one couple all along. In addition, many in Finland and abroad have said that our lives are already like a finished book or a script for a TV series or film. It is only now that everything is safely behind us that I have had the time and opportunity to write about our experiences.

What can I say about all this? I've created some kind of elevator talk about everything when I've met acquaintances while taking the dog out or answered the question at work events: "How are you? What you've been up to?". In return, I get reactions from spontaneous laughter to primitive crying. Many are horrified and startled. Most of the time, in the end I finally see a genuine empathetic stagnant gaze and a waiting face "What are you going to tell me next?". I've learned to get out of awkward silence by saying some casual comment that yes, we will get up again. Better quality of situation comics are more of my husband's hay.

The book describes the true events and situations of our own lives as we have experienced and sensed them - seen, heard and felt them.

EVERYTHING BEGINS WITH BLOOD

People are willing to go far to protect their secrets.

Crime writer Arttu Tuominen

The pool of blood from which I woke up has wrapped my long hair in its red cloak. At first, I can only try to open my eyes, but I only see a fog. It's humming in my head. I want to understand what happened and what will happen next. I can't understand what has happened and why? I try to ask, but I can't even make a sound. The dizzying feeling competes with the incisive pain for power over me. The stone floor is cold and wet. Where does all this blood come from?

I have time to think about it when my consciousness clears momentarily. I feel a warm trembling hand stroking my cheek quietly. All my clothes are covered in the blood and cling to my skin like glue. I'm trying to turn around. "Don't get up, you can't!" A strict command strikes my consciousness. I don't even seem to be able to move, I find all the strength in my body is gone and a painful, overwhelming feeling fills my whole body. I try to focus on breathing. Someone raises my head and puts something under my head to keep my head from freezing on an ice-cold tile floor.

The blood is coming out with an accelerating force that I can barely stay conscious. Suddenly I hear my husband shout on the phone, "Where is that ambulance? She will bleed to death!". Blood pulps with force. Sometimes my vision turns black and occasionally I see blurry characters around me in the brightness of the hallway lamps. The open front door brings in cold air, even though the April nights are already getting warmer with caution. Nature is opening its eyes towards spring, but can I still see this spring? No birds are singing. Not now. Or at least I can't hear anything from the outside. I distinguish a character who speaks quietly to themselves, "As if someone had been murdered."

I hear the sound of sirens. Outside, my husband's waving hands reflect a blue flashing light. The sounds of the sirens are amplifying and approaching. The ambulance stops and paramedics arrive. They kneel and start treating me with pace. "1.3 litres of blood have already been lost." "Life threatening, she must be taken to hospital urgently." I hear individual sentences from a distance when I am lifted on my stretcher. "We don't know how it will go, she has lost and continues to lose so much blood. We do our best", the paramedics say to my shocked husband Petri as they leave.

Memories are flimsy. Everything is like a dark cloud in my head. I am quickly transferred to an ambulance. Petri will have to prepare for the worst. The bleeding turns into like water balloons that explode when dropped on a stretcher. The sirens are ringing, and the ambulance is accelerating at full speed. My dad sits completely quiet in the front seat of the ambulance and holds the door handle with all his might.

I feel bounces on the road, but there's nothing I can do to prevent things from happening. The person behind me is talking to Jorvi Hospital on the phone: "Can't we get there? The situation is extremely serious, do we really have to go to another hospital?". He shouts in disbelief to the front seat that we are going to the hospital in Helsinki! The blood pressure is 75/44 and blood is still pushing out from inside. I hear the nurse's intensified conversation on the radio: "The caesarean section that is starting in the operating room must be stopped immediately or the patient arriving on our way dies."

US TWO

Hopes and Dreams

Years before when everything still was well.

– We can get sunscreen from there too, we need to go or we will be late. I am yelling annoyed from the front door.

Petri, as usual, calmly checks his list to make sure everything is in order. I pull heavy bags down the stairs. We live on the first floor, but still need to go down the stairs to the floor leading out. What type of fool designed the elevator like this! Finally, Petri gets in a taxi. I say: - To the airport. It is finally starting to feel like a vacation. No work or study for a week. When we arrive at the airport, my dad's uncle is already in line with his harmonica. More family and relatives arrive, and the atmosphere is happy. We are going to celebrate my mother's birthday in the Canary Islands. It's wonderful when both of my grandfathers are involved, they've become even closer friends after they both become widows too early. As we sit down on the plane, I look at my cousin with her adorable child. I want kids one day myself. This 8-year-old brisk girl was a flower girl at our wedding. Our wedding was less than a year ago. I lean back, close my eyes, and return to those moments.

Before I was born, my parents had given a name for a girl and a boy for emergency baptism as the old days they used to do, the boy's name would have been Petri. On Saturday, July 2001, they got Petri as a son-in-law in a yellow wooden church on the countryside, in the landscape of my parents' childhood. A couple of summers earlier on the churchyard bench, Petri had traditionally knelt romantically and asked:
– Will you marry me in this church?
I had been sitting in the same church on Christmas worship, my father dragged us there in the frost under the blanket with a sledge. Our wedding church reminds us of many good memories of our grandmothers, who were already buried in the churchyard at the time of our wedding.
I was full of energy when planning the wedding. On the day of the wedding, I noticed that I had lost weight and the dress was now too big. Fortunately, there were strings behind the dress that we could tighten it up. We had a lovely flower girl and a boy for whom we had bought the appropriate outfits. It was all like from a fairy tale when we got on horse-drawn carriages with them at our Country Wedding. The priest was Petri's friend - an aikido teacher who contributed to a relaxed and comfortable atmosphere for the wedding.
I arrived at church with horse-drawn carriages and my father escorted me to the altar where Petri was waiting with a gentle smile. Petri was so handsome in his suit. I looked at Petri and hoped that he would never change, but would always remain as he is now, gentle, faithful, uplifting, curious, a steady builder of life. As I stood at the altar, I thought of the words of the popular Finnish song "I got

everything from life". As we stood side by side, we looked at each other. We said our I Do's, wows and promised to support each other until death. Standing side by side, hand in hand, we didn't yet know how much we would have to change, dare, and squeeze each other's hands harder, and in difficult moments, find the will to continue together to get everything we dreamed of in life. Nothing came easily.

We left with the flower children from the church to the white mansion where the wedding ceremony was held. Petri's father said at the wedding that he was so happy when I changed my last name to my husband's name. There aren't many people named Nuora in Finland. He also wished us to have children to have more Nuoras. That is what we hope too.

Petri trampled his foot at the pace of the first cake cut - straight on my toes. In Finnish tradition it is believed that which of the bride and groom is the first to step on the floor during the cutting of the cake, has the final say on future decisions in the joint household. The wedding waltz succeeded with a sore foot in a modern style. We were dancing in multiple weddings in that summer when our circle of friends under thirty got married.

After the wedding party, we set off by car to spend the wedding night at a cabin in wilderness that we rented, which was hard to find. We drove for hours along the plains. Navigators were not yet standard equipment, and smartphones with map applications were not yet on the market. Eventually, I was ready to give up and sleep my wedding night on the back seat of my dad's car, after all it was a warm summer. Petri however did not give up and eventually a place was found. The same unyielding and on the other hand relaxation we would both need several times later in our marriage. On the wedding day, it really felt like nothing could ruin our happiness. And it didn't break, but the future cracks in life were so great that the rising of the water onto the ice could no longer be prevented. I learned that we need to move faster on the points where the ice still carries.

Start of our marriage was a wonderful time. We were curious to try many new things and challenge ourselves. Petri who was constantly assessing risks and trying to avoid high places, would never have thought of voluntarily jumping from a fully operational plane until his stag party took him to parachuting from four kilometres. Based on the training before the jump, he was able to state that sometimes you just have to go and have trust. For the other time, I was able to lure Petri, who is scared horses, to horse riding. The excitement was triggered at the latest when the horse had decided to move out to a bush along the route to feed. When Peter realized he had no way to control the horse, he decided to hold on tight and go where the muzzle shows and enjoy the sun and scenery - even then in the bush.

We were looking for a common hobby. The salsa started moving smoothly, but somewhere at the double helicopter spin, we both ran out of coordination. Golf sounded nice, after all, it includes a lot of outdoors and walks in the manicured park areas. However, the first hour of golf lessons, showed that my "swing" didn't fly a small ball further than a couple of feet. Eventually, the making of children, would become an activity that will fill all our free time.

We often talk about the future and have a dream in common: we want a big family. In addition to biological children, we would like to adopt children. We hope to have four children as the four clover of happiness. We think two of them would be adopted from abroad. We don't know much yet of adoption process.

In the early days of marriage, life flowed with its own weight. Studies progressed, we both got caught up in working life, we got a dog, we were young, healthy and happy. We enjoyed our lives and planned to get our careers off to a good start and to travel before children. Children are made "later sometime in our thirties". We had progressed to this stage in our life together quickly so now it could be slow down a little.

One Friday in October of 2002, we were headed to a nearby mall to buy groceries for the evening, as usual. Along the way, we realised we were exhausted and instead of shopping at the nearby grocery store in shopping centre Myyrmanni, we decided to change the evening menu to Chinese takeaway from the pickup restaurant on the outside wall of the shopping mall Iso-Myyri that is next to Myyrmanni. We walked home with the food and just when we got home, we heard on the TV news about the bomb that exploded in Myyrmanni. Right in the vicinity of the grocery store checkouts. Seven people lost their lives and nearly 200 were injured. The perpetrator was also among those who died. It felt bad to think of the pain of all the families who died and were injured and those close to them. Many lives ended too early.

Sun and fire

I wake up when the flight attendant announces the plane approaching Gran Canaria. I have managed to sleep almost the entire flight. The holiday seems to be coming for a good moment, I need a rest. The travel agency's shuttle bus takes us to a lovely hotel, where our party has rooms around the pool in a terraced house. It's nice to have fun and play with my cousin's little girl. After swimming I watch from the sun lounger at the sky. No clouds visible. Feeling relaxed, almost as carefree as being in Spain as a child with our parents. I remember our trips to a parrot park where a parrot stole my sister's earring from the ear without us noticing. I remember camel rides, lovely moments on the beach and the hotel's pools connecting the water slides - and lots of ice cream. My childhood is full of happy memories.

I was born in the mid-70s in Vantaa, near Helsinki. Everywhere at the time, new concrete suburbs arose to meet the needs of those moving from the country to the city. A blond-headed boy was born to the Nuora's family at the beginning of the year, and a girl with thick dark hair in Koivisto's family just before Christmas. When the children started school in 1983, our family lived in a quiet area, surrounded with parks, on a detached house in Espoo. Under the apple trees, we did plays and dances with my little sister and the kids in the neighbourhood, we were as free as the birds in the sky. We pick berries from the bushes in the hope of pocket money and play trade. Our home was at the back of the yard, a light green detached house built in the 1950s. There was a light green playhouse in the yard. On the edge of the yard grew rhubarbs, which our mom made wonderful pies with vanilla sauce. As a child, we also got to sweep sweat when we mowed the lawn or watered the flowers until late at night. We learn to work and be entrepreneurial when we are little. We had strong supporting community, and sometimes we got pocket money from the hard work at the kiosk.

My parents decided to extend our house. The construction project had a joyful spirit of making, from early in the morning to late nights, in the middle of the ongoing work. As the house was built, the timbers lifted us children during breaks in the long days of construction with a brick elevator to the roof, and it was a favourite activity for the entire neighbourhood kids. Life was relaxed, it didn't always have to be "just right", and we slept happily in the middle of dozens of sawdust sacks coming from the walls of an old house, in sleeping bags on camping pads covering a cement floor. The atmosphere on the street was like from the desperate housewives - series with children's games and a village parties. Later, as we grew older, shrubs and apple trees gave way to the houses to be built for me and my sister.

I get up to sit in a sun lounger when my skin starts to burn. I watch kids playing with a beach ball. I have always liked to hang out with the little ones. As a teenager, I was a team leader for a scout group for the smaller ones. Together with other kids of my age, we organized trips to outdoor camping area for the little ones, where our flagship cabin was located near the lake. There were no adults involved in the trip, so us, the older kids, had a responsibility for the smaller ones. I was only 12 years old. It seemed natural and I was not afraid of responsibility, because my childhood in Finland did not have seat belts in cars, and no one had heard of a cycling helmet. It was all dangerously carefree. At most, the major challenge was getting a rain inside of the tent while camping and waking up in a large pool of water. However, once during our stay in a familiar scout cabin, some disturbing young people appeared outside the cottage. We had almost ten small children with us and there were only a few of us older children. The teenagers set fire to the tree next to the cottage to scare us. That's when I was really scared because we were so far from the town on our own without adults. For the first time, I was responsible for young children in a threatening situation.

I wake up to the point where my skin burns soon, I need to put in more sunscreen. It's already afternoon, but the sun is hot. The day will soon turn into evening. Fortunately, I can swim this trip since it's not "that time of the month". I usually suffer from heavy menstruation, and my endometriosis gets worse at an accelerating rate. I know it's a risk to infertility. Endometriosis is a condition where tissue similar to the lining of the womb starts to grow in other places, such as the ovaries and fallopian tubes, causing a chronic inflammatory reaction in the tissue. Among other things, it causes infertility. It is one of the most common gynecological diseases in the world, with up to one in ten women suffering from endometriosis. Due to the difficulty in diagnosing the disease, the diagnosis may take several years, which may be critical years in infertility care for couples dreaming of a child. Fortunately, I have been diagnosed at a young age, so I know there is no time to waste.

The desire for children has been strengthened throughout our time together, and we have begun to mentally begin to start a family before it is too late. Before the trip to Spain, we bought our own apartment in Martinlaakso, close enough of Helsinki. Our apartment has two bedrooms. The office room would turn into a children's room when the time came. The only annoyance is smoking a neighbour on his balcony. In the cool of the evening, he somehow gets a bitter smell on our balcony too, and we get to start each morning by ventilating the smoke from our own balcony. I would never smoke tobacco.

Whether it's the dark nights and warm air of Spain, or an uninterrupted spending time together with Petri, but after just a couple of nights, we decide to start trying to get pregnant. The studies are still in progress, but we will have time to finish them on maternity leave while the child is sleeping. My endometriosis has already become painful at this point, so it's a good idea to start trying to have a baby fast. Because only one of our friends has a child and we are on the move quite early in relation to our circle of friends, we are spared from the curiosity of starting family. Now we are still safe from the interviewers.

Breakdown

Spring turns into summer and summer into August. The cycles wear out, but the pregnancy does not begin. We should go for investigations now. Everything is definitely fine, it doesn't always instantly work out. However, Petri starts looking for infertility clinic numbers. In a few days later, we are already sitting in the white corridor of the clinic. I look at the adorable picture of the baby on the wall in her parents 'arms at the same time Petri might be looking at something completely different while giving the sample. I wish we had a baby. Not everything happens fast, but I still have a strong belief that things will get better, as Grandma always said. We would still succeed. Now we will just get a little assurance that everything is going well. I press a leaking wound in my forearm from laboratory tests. Petri comes out of the sampling room a little embarrassed with a grin. "It is indeed easier that there is a stand for that magazine provided by the clinic, you would run out of hands". We both laugh. - Your results will come in a week, the nurse shouts after us as, we leave towards the door with a smile.

Friday. Evening at home alone. "I travel to my feelings, to my innermost being" The theme song of the popular Finnish TV series takes me to the imaginary everyday life of others and its exciting situations. All things that can happen to others. After the program, I browse through the channels, but comedies or crime scene investigators don't bring comfort to a lonely evening. Petri is gone all night. He has a training day, after which the work crew heads to the evening together. It would have made sense for me, too, to plan something for the evening, but the work and studies took me a whole week. My gaze shifts to our framed wedding picture standing on a shelf on TV. Everything was like a fairy tale with horse-drawn carriages. Suddenly I get shivers. It's kind of cold, even though the August night has been warm. I close the balcony door, the neighbour has smoked again. I look at the yard and I see a strange dark dressed figure, an older woman staring intently in the yard towards me. This place doesn't feel like home for our future family. I find strange people living here. I lock the balcony door.

I jumped over the pile of mail when I got home. Petri usually scrolls through the mail when he comes home, but while he's at work, the pile still hangs in front of the door. I reach down to pick up a bunch of ads and notice a letter from an infertility clinic under them. I have promised Petri that whatever they found, we would not share the results with others until we had gone through it together. Can I open the letter alone, is it worth it? Fear tries to take over, but I decide to ignore it. Why would I be afraid for nothing? There is nothing to lose here. Even if there would be some minor issues, it will definitely be fine. I open the letter and its contents are shocking. In disbelief, I read the lines over and over again: I couldn't get pregnant normally in any way, possibly not at all. The letter is so surprising that to my shock I don't know what to do. It feels like a rope is strangling my neck. The mental pressure feels like that what I saw outside earlier that elderly woman with black cloths, hair in tight bun would be right in front of me, that cruel-looking woman. Her evil grin wants misfortune for us, for us to fail. It wasn't the hippopotamus that came to our home, to our living room, but this dark figure stepped into the bedroom and every place in our home. I try to shake the embodiment of my fears out of my mind.

The loop tightens. I need to talk to someone right away. I can't reach Petri today. I can't talk to my friends or family yet. In distress I call to number inquiry services.

- Can you connect to a crisis phone, or whatever they are called? I manage to ask from surprised woman.

- I could connect you to local crisis line. She kindly suggests. There then. A gentle male voice answers my call and asks how he can help me. I burst into tears, and I can't say anything.

- Take your own time, I be here, has something happened? He asks.

- I don't know if I ever will be a mother. That's the only thing I manage to say and I keep crying: -I want so much a child, children and to be mother for them.

The man answers calmy: -You know, let me tell you about my neighbours. They too, hoped for a child for a longest time and now they have a small little girl from China. They are truly happy to finally be parents. I keep crying, but the shock has turned into hope from hysteria. I thank the man for telling me about the adopted child. Yes, I will still be a mother. Some day. One way or another.

From that letter begins the second phase of my life. Nothing is as it used to be, but I will not give up. I've always wanted to be a mom, and I refuse to let go of my dream and role. The role of a kind girl and motherhood is part of me, but now it's time to fight. I have had the courage to act since I was a little scout, but in this situation I am helpless. In the scouts, I would have just safely made a knot on the string and attached a shed or raft with it, but now the whole string has slipped out of hand.

Everything in my life was clear but now nothing is clear anymore, I can't function without a clear goal. I ascend to the boxing ring and face a dark-looking figure. The joy in my eyes has turned into bitter anger. I will win this match no matter what it takes. The briskness and freedom of the little girl I once was, has now changed to purposeful advancement in heavy chains. My smile on my face is no longer genuine, it's a secret shell, mandatory accessory to be able to go to work. I decide that one day I will still tear the shell off my face and rejoice with my children, feeling the smell of grass and apple tree flowers without this heavy feeling in my chest. That day is not today, but it will come. The day is not yet visible on the calendar. However, that day is marked on the calendar of my life with a star and a heart.

We are a family without children. Our way of life is built on home-centred activities suitable for children. Only the children are missing. We have to come up with something. I will find out everything there is to know about adoption from relative organisations. I would find out about adopting every possible child from adoption organizations. I want to gain hope by exploring this path while allowing future infertility treatments to go their own way. I try to be relaxed even when I can't. I can't stop now. Suddenly the focus of our lives has changed. Starting a family would now be expensive. The idea of two of us traveling together and postpone a having a child has changed to researching our options with doctors and adoption organisations. It also drives to forced performance at work to advance a career to cover the cost of having a child.

The next morning, I call the Infertility Clinic to find out how to proceed based on these results.

- Just make an appointment with our doctor and he will advise you ahead. That's what I do. In the evening we will tell the situation to both of our families. Everyone listens seriously and it is clear to everyone that we have not come to lose this match. We give faith to others, even though when the door closes, we are like two swans stuck in the mud, tapping together desperately but faithfully next to each other.

We tell about our situation in work and to our circle of friends. I more openly, Petri cautiously only to a few, afraid of people's reactions. A friend of mine had bought a large station wagon soon after their wedding. At the time I bluntly commented if they are expecting to have children in near future. I heard from them later that they are having infertility treatments. It is this same friend who is now advising us to an infertility clinic where they themselves are getting their treatments. The results there are good, and even difficult cases can be handled according to individual needs. I am grateful to my friend. One should never inquire or assume anything about the lives of others but listen with an open heart to what the other wants to say and offer help.

I

Two lines
Radiating that night
In a freshly painted house
There was no need to worry about debts or anything
With a newly assembled bed
With sheets fresh from package
You whispered to me in your smile
Now we make a child
And we did
Six angels later[1]

Race

In the hallway of the infertility clinic, I see a lot of women of different ages. Some of them are happy, others are hopeful, some are excited, someone is wiping their crying eyes at the end of the hallway. I also see men in the clinic, someone is supporting their wife, another is going to the reception.

Everyone has a common desire for a child. I wonder what the story of everyone is. I notice the stroller and hear the baby's voice. It affects everyone in the hallway. At first, I startle, shocked at how someone dares to bring the child here. I soon realize she has an equal concern for her own situation. She probably hopes for a sibling for her child and suffers from secondary infertility when, for one reason or another, they do not succeed in having a other child.

A friend of mine said that there are queues on the public side and the number of infertility treatments and forms of treatment is limited. After doing some research I understand that with the public offering we would not win the race against endometriosis. I can't wait, I definitely need the full range of treatments in all their forms before the child is safely napping on the balcony. (Finland it is common practise to put your baby outside to sleep during the day, were it summer or winter)

The doctor is gently explaining how the process is going. First an attempt is made to get the menstrual cycle in order, followed by insemination and then, if necessary, punctures and in vitro fertilization. After each, there would always be something to try. Yes, one of them will succeed, I think hopefully. However, I know couples for whom no treatment has helped. I brush the thought off my mind, only this next stage is what is important. When I'm not in the clinic, I try to reset my head with light TV series. I feel like I am running a nonstop marathon with my body, which isn't really at the level of a top athlete. Or as if I were in a formula race where everything happens quickly with the help of a professional team and all I must do is drive and manage to stay on the road to my destination. As long as I survive to the next service point or depot, there will again be the next energy boost or better tuning that will try to help me to advance to the next stage. During and after treatment, it feels like I'm being beaten in a boxing ring. Hormones are confusing me. They cause irritation, exhaustion, and a roller coaster of emotions.

I am so pain sensitive and I am afraid of puncturing at first so much that I have to be put to sleep. The nurses and doctors are friendly and live with our pain. When I wake up, Petri sits in a chair next to the bed and the nurse brings the crackers with melted cheese. - There were a lot of eggs found, surely some will be fertilized and we will be able to move them inside you, the doctor will tell you in more detail. The nurse encourages. Fortunately, there are a lot of eggs. We are excited about their development and look forward to the day when they could be moved.

You must drink a lot on the day of embryo transfer. I came with a bubble on the forehead and with a bladder full for the best visibility for the procedure. I rumble in like an elephant-sized water balloon on a lumpy road. The stairs are painful to climb. I want to do everything perfectly so that under no circumstances I could blame myself if things go wrong. The chances of success are so low anyway. This trait always lives in me strongly: let's get things done and do everything we can, so we don't have to think about what else we could have done afterwards. I lean against the wall in pain and wait for the procedure to begin. I come into the room and the doctor puts the tube inside and transfer begins.

- Is it ready there? The nurse looks at cell biologist.
- Yes, here they come. The answer comes from behind the glass.

My children. Two embryos are transferred inside me under ultrasound control. There are risks in both, single and dual embryo transfer. I wish even the other one survived. I look at the screen and see small flashes. Maybe there would be twins. Twin pregnancy increases and at the same time decreases the chances of success. After discussing with the doctors, it becomes clear that two embryos are better for me to succeed.

13 lines and drops

Monday. It has been now two weeks since the embryos were transferred, and we are able to take a pregnancy test. We sit excited in the bathroom.

- Well, now we can look. Petri checks time solemnly. Two lines! From the bottom of our hearts, we cry in each other's embrace when the test is positive. The lines aren't strong, but for us, that's enough right now. We leave happily and in disbelief to the mall. We try to look smart and that we have a plan on the outside, but now even Petri's systematicity has for a momentarily evaporated into non-existent with the autumn leaves: - Let's buy that pregnancy seat belt, to protect the baby and you.

I focus on the cute little socks I would slip the baby's feet into. When uphill has been steep enough, the subsequent hill will take us again at such a rapid pace that the brakes cannot be applied. The only thing we have hoped for from the beginning would be just normal ordinary everyday life, which is now perhaps finally within our reach. Nothing could break our happiness anymore.

Blood. After a couple of weeks, I sit in the bathroom again. Petri talks to the infertility clinic on the phone. The nurse instructs:

- Bleeding may be normal in a well-progressing pregnancy as well. Come here and lets take a pregnancy hormone value and check the situation. When I come out of the lab, I feel disbelieving. How does this end? I drive to my work's parking lot and wait in the car. The phone rings and the nurse's words cross my consciousness: - The value is too low for the pregnancy to continue, I'm sorry. The matter itself is crushing. It feels hard to know that we can't normally try to get pregnant again, but there are infertility treatments and a hormone storm ahead again. I look with empty eyes at the last leaves falling to the ground. They disappear with the water into the sewer. Winter is coming.

After the first miscarriage, I stop looking at the screen of the ultrasound device. My own infertility doctor already knows this, but sometimes when other doctors examine me at a women's clinic, for example, the doctor may tell me: - Look how great it is now, your child is there, why don't you look?

In the end, I am too tired to explain anymore. I just don't look. I want to keep my distance mentally to protect myself. After the first miscarriage, the joy of anticipation has disappeared and turned into a terrified fear, which I am fighting with a rational cover of a contingency plan, a plan for the next step ready in my other hand. Failed attempts. Miscarriages. Always a new plan and attempt. Positive lines in pregnancy test. Excited days and weeks. Cautious wish. Disappointments. Horror. Drops of blood. Despair. I decide to stop counting miscarriages. I just can't take it anymore. There are already too many of them. If anyone asks, I'll just say some number that's roughly correct. Thirteen is a good number, the number of misfortunes. I will continue the treatments.

It's evening. I'm trying to fall asleep. The old nasty woman from the horror movie is in the corner of the bedroom disturbing my sleep and wishing everything would go wrong again. Miscarriages are sometimes lightly written about in the newspapers. Having experienced the brutality of a miscarriage myself physically and mentally, I find that its scope and depth often do not fit into a single article. There is so much pain and horror associated with miscarriages. We have not been allowed to be parents and have no memories of our child or our time as a family. Sure, there is always that short or sometimes a little longer moment when I'm pregnant, but the fear of losing has taken away the joy from that too. I stare at the roof. Miscarriage is death. The child has been loaded with expectations and wishes. Everything is going to fall apart. Bottomless emptiness. We start from scratch to try again. Willpower must be found somewhere, somehow, we have to move forward. It feels bad to hear encouraging comments: - Its going to be fine, just attempt again.

The intension is good of course, everyone means well and wish to encourage us to move forward. However, we are still in a period of mourning from the previous loss, but we have no time to mourn. We are like robots in the starting racks, forced to advance in the race. Endometriosis is running in front of us, we can't stop crying now. It's really tough not to be able to be a parent for your child even a minute, even though you haven't wished for anything else in your life.

We have moved farther out of town, to a place where there is room to breathe and a small yard where we can put baby to sleep when the time comes. I sit outside on the terrace of our home and try to recover from one miscarriage again. The losses are overwhelming, but there have been them in my life, even before infertility. Looking back at an empty yard, I return to my memories of the painful situations of the past. I see them in front of me as I did then. My safe worldview was shaken properly in our home for the first time when I was 11, when my dad came home from work and didn't even come in through the door but went straight out into the basement to cry. My mother ran to help, and my little sister and I sneaked into the basement stairs to secretly listen. I saw my father in my mother's arms, in despair, while my mother comforted him. The parents noticed us and asked us to come closer. Our dear grandmother, my father's mother, had had a seizure and the situation was serious. That's when I first realized that nothing in life is certain or permanent - nothing.

The most shocking moments in my childhood and youth were the premature deaths of both grandmothers to diseases and the accidental death of my close friend in a car accident. The surprising nature of the car accident brought out the different ways in which people react to shock. Some people want to mourn alone, for others it is important to go through the situations continuously, some deal with the matter through memories, others fully investing in the funeral. For me, after the initial feelings of horror and disbelief have faded a little, it was important to talk about it when reality hit me in the face. I talked about my grief with my friend as we walked countless miles. We talked and remembered all the good moments of our friend and on the other hand we mourned the fate of our friend, how she would have had so much left to live. It is unfair that too many people don't get the chance to live all the stages of life that everyone should be granted.

The series of shocking incidents also included a traffic accident in our village, where a small schoolchild was hit by a car. I happened to be there when the shocked mother, tried to tear herself away from the grip of the policemen who had come to the scene, to help her child while the paramedics tried in vain to save the child's life. Love for a child is something so great.

Due to events in my childhood, I have a huge fear of losing people to accidents and illnesses. I'm afraid of getting sick myself because of its severity. My fear was triggered by a tough job at the dawn of adulthood. I was supposed to go take care of children through an association, but they urgently needed a substitute carer for a young man suffering from muscular dystrophy. The man had been ill for several years and was lifted by a crane.

- You will be trained for the job when you get there. The association's contact person encouraged. My mother warned that the work could be tough, she was worried about how the events would affect me: - You are too young for that job. However, selflessness and the desire to help overcame my worries, and so I decided to accept the job. I arrived at the agreed time at the house where the man's parents were leaving for an important meeting. They advised me, left, and the patient and I were left alone. The man could not speak. I took care of the visit according to the instructions and everything went well. The man's fate touched me very much, I cried the whole way while cycling home. The man's parents were satisfied and asked me to continue taking care of their son. I absolutely wanted to help and decided to toughen myself up.

One sunny day, I had cycled to the patient's home again. There was a lot of time left after the treatments, and the man wasn't tired today. I had time to read the entire day's newspaper to him. "We still have time left together, I could get a book from that shelf and read it to you". I had to make the decisions for him, because he was no longer able to express his will even with gestures. I was reading a book to him in their garden and suddenly noticed that his eyes were starting to close. I laughed and said: - I guess this book is a bit boring and a bad choice. Surprisingly, he said: - Yeah.

The man moved excitedly as he realized that he could answer and his condition suddenly improved. I immediately called his parents, who delighted came home straight away and called the doctors. The man was transferred to the hospital so that his good condition could be examined and promoted. I was happy and thought that everything is possible in life. The hope remained for a long time, but unfortunately the man did not see the next Christmas. His fate remains in my memories and fears.

A faint breeze shakes me from my memories, and I look at the cloudless sky. With the memories of these deaths, I pondered the question of why good people die? It feels so unfair, but you can't divide people - everyone are good people, valuable from the moment they are born. When I was young, I thought a lot about how to support people when the very smooth path of life starts to turn in a harmful direction when the mind is disturbed. I myself try to keep my mind together in such a way that when every new attempt starts, plan B is ready. If only I could immediately start implementing the next plan, I might be able to bear the probable loss better. In the midst of losses, the best support is genuinely caring, listening and an empathetic desire to find a solution to the situation together. Sometimes the solution can also be a time-out with a chocolate bar.

Petri and I decide to do something fun between treatments. Even before the infertility treatments, we went on short and longer trips together. Petri has been a great partner in all our adventures. We met for the first time at the coffee shop of the University of Helsinki's Southern Finns department. I was working as an assistant hostess, and Petri was a returnee after the army to become a student. Petri had had a more carefree life than me, even though he had experienced losses too. However, Petri had managed to develop a "Chin to chest and towards new adversities" attitude towards life. Petri's everyday life revolved around his aikido hobby and life smiled for him. For Petri, school had gone easily without requiring too much work. He had subjects of interest, but not many plans for the future. Still, he didn't worry too much: - Things will work out as intended.

We were friends at first and it seemed to me that nothing could hurt Petri. However, he could not have imagined what a wild adventure he would end up in when he left the student party in the evening to escort me to the bus stop.

Our friendship quickly deepened into love and after a short courtship we concluded that we wanted to spend all our time together and moved in together. The start of our life together was busy time in amidst studies and work in our first small home in Espoo's Tapiola. I walked home with shopping bags to an old, idyllic area of small apartment buildings, where the quiet life of retirees, students and others was only interrupted by the customers from the local small pub and their loud search for taxis going home. Our life together started here. I lived in the apartment alone at first, but already the following year from our first meeting, Petri carried his aikido uniforms and other things to my little apartment, which didn't have a balcony. A balcony would have made it easier to air out the aikido suits after training (huh!). The suits were aired in the same small bathroom where we showered. We used a closet to divide half of the studio into a bedroom, and at the end was a small table with chairs in front of a large window. A kitchen recess and a small wardrobe, and that was the whole apartment. Life there was happy.

School and work took most of our time. The little time off we had, we wanted to travel, adventure and experience the world. We spend a lot of time outdoors. When going down the rapids of Kuusamo, it felt like an exciting amusement park device became a reality. The canoeing trip in Oulanka river was like a cross-section of our future lives: we tried to paddle in the same direction, but sometimes the canoe was sideways in the river, in the next moment we scrambled to the sand, sometimes one had to paddle for both of us, at the end we had to pick up our pace to get to our destination before dark. Communication in the canoe was colourful at times as Petri tried to guide us towards what he thought was the best route in the river, while I at the same time tried to paddle forward as fast as I could. In the end, the cooperation was successful, and after we finished, we had good memories of the trip. Just like in our marriage.

The most important thing in life is humility and passion.
Whatever you do,
do it like you had fire behind you.
Plunge into it with your body straight,
with two twists,
because only that way
you redeem your self-respect.
And if you fall, get up,
put a bind on the knee
and advance again.
And if you keep falling,
think that nobody
fall as handsomely as I do.
So handsome
straight to his stomach and vantage point.
For blessed are those who
who know how to laugh at themselves,
because they will not lack fun in their life. [2]

I have often returned to this poem in my thoughts and told others about it as an example of my attitude to life. I get through life's difficult and sad situations by laughing at my failures and trying not to take things too seriously. It is the only way I can get up and try again.

In the harsh wave of infertility treatments, it becomes a fun habit for us to start playing around, we take turns putting ourselves in a situation that is not typical for us, while the other person films the situation. Petri has his way with words, so as a master of situational comedy, he is usually the one who throws himself to be first try. Contrary to our customs, we impulsively leave for Rhodes without any plans. The place has been familiar to Petri since his childhood. After we got there, we explored the island's program offerings. Practicing Greek dances with Papa Ouzo sounds perfect for a try new thing- mission. Petri completes his Greek dance studies nicely at the village party and I try to film what I can with my laughter. However, I have to hold back my laughter and show that we are taking your dance studies seriously. Holding back a fit of laughter makes my eyes water. It's wonderful to "cry" laughter out. Petri's fan picture with Papa Ouzo is enough to bring laughter at the beach and on hikes for the whole week. If only we could return to this joy sometime.

Most of the time our lives are confined to our home. We close ourselves off from the outside world, afraid of seeing babies, struggling with pain, experiencing miscarriages and living in the middle of a constant secret. For some reason, my stomach swells visibly at the beginning of each treatment and I get smiling, questioning looks and even direct questions about whether we are possibly expecting a new member to the family. I can't handle those questions. Also, there is not much money except for treatments. We go to work and reset our heads in front of the TV with junk food in order to get up again for the next day. A friend of ours who is undergoing infertility treatments recommends the video rental store's comedy shelf to us, and we become regular customers of the rental store. We direct the attention and love reserved for children to our small dogs.

Miscarriages follow each other, they happen a lot, especially in early pregnancy. Mentally, we both deal with our grief in different ways and the ways to cope are also different. I'm the one who tries to drown myself in work and going out to forget about the reality. I can't stay at home; I always have to do something until I fall asleep from exhaustion. Instead, Petri wants to be at home, calm down and process everything. These ways of dealing with pain drive us apart, but they don't separate because we share the same goal. We are both committed to our plan and neither of us wants to give up. In these times, our marriage is a matter of will. We want to be together even when feelings and romance are buried under needles and medical bills.

Everyday life takes its own path on the side-lines, when the fierce goal of getting to the child takes the main role. Sometimes, Life visits us in a form of small cruises, but even then, I feel like I'm wearing a collar, someone other than me regulates my life. The moments of freedom are apparent, like small oases in an endlessly long desert, which allow you to move forward again for a while.

At times Petri suggests that we should go to a restaurant to eat and clear our heads, but I can't go. Every parent with their baby in a stroller makes me cry spontaneously, so forcing myself to stay at a restaurant table while eating is not possible. I could do something else; Petri wants to go home. We make comfort food at home in the evenings when I come home from lectures, and we watch Friends from the TV. It takes many episodes of Friends and other refreshments (read: chocolate, nachos and ice cream) to keep us fuelled for the next treatment session. It feels good to laugh at Friends for a while and to feel as if the wind has taken your worries to a warehouse, where you don't have to pick them up, at least today. As good friends as Ross and Rachel are becoming to us, it's impossible for me to watch episodes where they're expecting a baby and having kids.

My colleague is asking us to be his child's godparents and I would be the godmother. How could I stand it? My lovely co-worker knows about our pain of infertility, and I ask to meet the baby first and see if I could be a godmother. As an empath, she fully understands, and I go to meet the baby. It's scary to take the baby in my arms, I'm afraid I'll suffocate, but I'm also overcome with a feeling of great happiness. I am so happy to be a part of this child's life. I want them to be happy. I wish the same for all children in the world. Christmas day makes me nervous, but I'm happy. I hold the little one in my arms. We have agreed that if my condition worsens, my friend or Petri will take the baby. This is what did happen. I'm starting to get dizzy in the middle of baptisms. I lean against the wall behind me. Petri takes the baby quickly and the baptism continues. A few guests look questioningly at the situation. My friend's gentle accepting face and the little one's breathing calm me down.

Petri never refers to my appearance negatively. On the contrary, in all situations, he really sees behind my hip dips, spiked buttocks and chocolate-flecked skin and manages to remind me that I'm the perfect for him just the way I am. Tired, tearful, sometimes momentarily almost desperate. Also in pain when I can't do anything but lie down. In those moments Petri hugs and sees flashes of light. I need these moments so that I don't give up and just lie down in the dark. We are in this together like in a Finnish Poet Tommy Taberman's poem.

To commit so deeply
that becomes endless
Squeeze so hard
that becomes infinite
Loves so madly
that nothing more
be meaningless [3]

Try the truth

It's hard to manage work in middle of infertile treatments. However, financial security is an absolute prerequisite for us to be able to go through infertility treatments quickly. It's comforting that I still don't fully understand the desperate battle I'm waging against my body.

In hopes of becoming a teacher I applied to study pedagogy in faculty of education. However, as the turn of the millennium approached, I ended up developing e-learning environments as a pedagogue alongside my studies. From there, I moved to the IT field at the turn of the 21st century, when the industry began to need a lot of labour. There was talk of an IT bubble when the internet became popular rapidly in the mid-1990s. Hype was born with it, which was, however, followed by the financial overvaluation of the information technology industry and eventually a collapse. With my educational background, in my work in the IT field, I am constantly learning new things, and I especially like that I get to design together with client's solutions that promote their line of work and learning. I persevere through projects, giving up is not an option when the announcement of the service is the next morning.

The workload in IT and constant secrecy are draining my energy resources. I don't want to tell everyone, that I am pregnant and that I have to refuse wine and certain foods. I want to ensure that a possible pregnancy has even a small chance of success. A small circle at work what is really happening and why I am constantly at the doctor. They and everyone we trust form a seamless safety ring around us, which protects us from hurtful curiosity: - Have you already planned to start a family?

The comments would make me collapse, but the secret, empathetic, friendly looks of the colleagues who know about the situation give me strength and I answer: - Everything in a good time, of course we dream of children, but they will come sometime.

In my thoughts, the sentence continues: - From somewhere. Somehow.

We don't really have time together anymore when we are constantly worried about the risk of not having a family. We will get together sometime in the future. I suffer from the fatigue and limitations of constant early pregnancies, Petri tries to support me, but is alone a lot when I sleep.

Petri is afraid to tell at work where he often disappears in the middle of the working day for a few hours. I am trying to encourage Petri to tell. In the end, when he finally has courage to tell others, everyone at work supports and understands him. People are benevolent when they know what's going on in the background. The support from both employers is always strong. When you tell things openly, you can be yourself everywhere. Petri's trusted long-term team leader summed it up well: - When no other explanation helps, it's good to try the truth. This is how we decide to always act in the future.

I am fully involved in the treatment schedules. The calendar is filled with important dates and reservations. If only I can endure these, then our luck will turn again.

From ditch to flight

The next attempt. Everything is going according to the plan until the pregnancy test. This time, the test will be done in a clinic instead of testing at home, so that the hormone value can be confirmed immediately. It's high. We don't celebrate it. I'm just telling Petri that things are progressing again. He replies that we will wait. Nothing else. Neither of us can believe that we are going to be parents anymore. Only when the child is actually in our arms with little socks on his feet then would we believe it.

Pregnancy progresses week by week. I go to work. In my free time, I mostly rest or go for leisurely walks as I feel tired all the time. That should be a good sign. One morning I'm in the client's auditorium

40

getting ready to give a lecture. There are at least a hundred people there. Everyone is ready for my presentation, and I should start the lecture in 15 minutes. People are walking in, and I greet them as they come. Suddenly I feel a strange pain in my lower abdomen and at the same time it seems like bleeding. I leave instantly to the women's room. In the toilet, I undress, sit down and before I can do anything, I miscarry. Everything comes out. There is nothing unclear about that. I'm so shocked from the sadness of the loss, but I'm trying to think fast how I'm going to get through this lecture. What would I say when I entered the auditorium? I am holding back my tears and try to pull myself together. I feel that in this moment that I can't grieve right now, not there, I just have to put it out of my mind now. I stuff my pants full of pads and stagger out of the booth. I look at myself in the mirror. I look like a ghost. I don't know what else to do but quickly throw cold water on my face. I dry my face and quickly fix my makeup. My head and eyes hurts, I want to cry, but I brace myself, stand up straight and head towards the hall: - I'll go and give that lecture and then we'll see what happens.

I enter the hall as people turn to look in my direction. Fortunately, the lecture hall is already dimmed for my presentation. I slip through the darkness to the speaker's place, take a deep breath, clear my mind and start my speech. Words and presentation slides transfer me to another reality. Apparently, something sensible has come out of my mouth when I notice that the hour has passed, and the audience is clapping happily.

- It was a good presentation, thank you very much. The customer's representative is happy.

- Would you like to go to lunch with us to continue the discussion on the topic? My colleague looks at me questioningly and smiles.

- Unfortunately, I have another meeting in my calendar right after, I have to hurry. I answer kindly and smile.

I leave quickly and run outside. There is no next meeting. I run until I'm sure I'm far enough that none of the participants from the presentation can see me. My legs fail me, and I fall into the ditch. My long hair gets caught in a bush growing in the ditch. I cry everything out, absolutely everything, all the failed pregnancies that I haven't had time to mourn. I can't hold it in anymore. Through despair, the cry eventually turns into a mournful sob and a sad self-surprise. I'm in a ditch now. At least, I can experience nature at close range, all the smells of the ditch penetrate my nose. My mind clears and I tear myself away from the bush and despair. It's time to take out plan B again and head towards the next attempt.

- I am literally at the bottom of the ditch. Can you pick me up? I ask from my mother on the phone.

- I'm going to come right away, it's a quick drive from here. My mother comforts. She pulls up in a moment, holds out her hand and takes me home. She doesn't need to ask what happened. Mom knows.

I am extremely grateful that my parents are alive and well in the middle of all this and that I have always been able to lean on them even in moments of despair. I would like to be the same kind of parent for my own children, but will I ever have them in my arms? Even the thought feels crushing. I can't give fear any space in my mind now, not even an inch.

When I was young, I crafted a clock with a picture of a fish as a gift for my father, on which I wrote "Happiness comes by searching, good catch by asking". I have learned from my father that I should never give up. The saying really went like this, that happiness doesn't come by looking for it, and good catch doesn't come by asking for it. I turned it around and realized that only with my own efforts could I achieve something, even in this most important project of my life. Instead of happiness, our guiding star is strengthened by unyieldingness. Our team does not sail by luck. We get information and try a lot of different treatment methods. We will not give up until we are a family.

Everything can be done.
Everything must be done.
All doors must be opened,
All moons to be reached.
There is only one condition,
lifeline:
A trembling soul must not be trampled upon.[5]

I have always wanted to be busy with children. It seems unfair that my chance to become a mother is taken away, but I soon realize that bitterness leads nowhere. We need to start thinking more broadly about it now. From the beginning, Petri and I have wanted four children, two babies and two children through adoption. There are many children in the world who are looking for parents and we are looking for children. We would just have to be united. Perhaps our way is for all our children to come through adoption. I'm going to look into it further and start talking about it at work. Surprisingly, there is a co-worker who is in the adoption queue with her husband. They could have a child soon. I get a lot of strength from the joy of their waiting, while I struggle with the treatments myself. I actively put aside thoughts about treatments and keep my mind fresh with the help of adoption. I learned a lot about adoption in Thailand and I think that maybe our child will arrive from there someday.

One bright, ordinary morning, my co-worker excitedly comes to my workstation and shows me a lovely picture: - Here is our child, now it's happening!

It's as if the clouds have all moved aside, forming an alley of honour, for the parents leaving to pick up their child home. A wonderful moment: - I am so happy for you.

After a few months, the happy family will arrive from Thailand to Finland. When the child has settled in well, Petri and I will have the opportunity to go meet this charming little boy. As we play with him, it becomes clear to us that adoption is also our path to becoming parents.

However, at the same time, the treatments continue like a never-ending train ride. I don't even know when I could mentally stop them. It's as if I've detached myself and my thoughts from the body, which hormones are pumped for treatments, and at the same time I'm already focusing in my mind on the fact that our child is waiting for us somewhere in the world.

- Let's at least try these remaining existing embryos now and then see what to do. I suggest to Petri and the last viable two embryos are transferred.

Once again, I'm pregnant, just like the previous times. This time, however, it takes longer than before. The bleeding doesn't start, even though I expect it every time I pull my pants down. Days pass, weeks pass. The situation looks pretty good for once. On top of everything, I have twins growing inside me, in the ultrasound the doctor sees two strong hearts! Would we dare to hope in success now? Despite the small hope, the familiar pattern repeats itself again. In the middle of a work meeting, I feel something start to flow. Not again! The bleeding tells with deadly accuracy that the attempt has failed this time as well. Fortunately, we hadn't put too many hopes into this last attempt, after all, we already have a plan for adoption. Supported by the sad expressions and slumped shoulders of my colleagues, I get into a taxi that will take me to the clinic. It's crushing to be in this situation again. A familiar doctor gives me an ultrasound: - With the miscarriage, the heartbeat is no longer visible. We will take a closer look at the uterus to make sure there is nothing left in the uterus that could cause problems for your health.

- I do not believe it! The doctor suddenly exclaims and continues: - There is a deformity in your uterus and there is a cavity where there is the beating heart of the second embryo we transferred! Your other twin is still fighting for his life! The doctor exclaims in disbelief. I try to ask: - Is it really true? Tears fall from my eyes. Hope and fear go hand in hand.

While I have lost my second child again and am mourning it, I rejoice that the other one is alive. I fear losing him too. Now begins an even bigger struggle and a consistent journey, where we will again do everything, we can, to get our little child out alive. All our energies must again be concentrated only on this.

> *"You miss 100 % of the shots you don't take"*
> ~~*Wayne Gretzky*~~ *Michael Scott*[5]

The motivational statement written on a flipchart by one of the main characters in the Office, American television series, is self-explanatory. If you don't try, you can't succeed.

Weeks pass. I ask the doctor: - Really?

- Yes. The doctor answers and continues: - Believe it already and look now, finally, after all the efforts here, baby is growing nicely!

- His name will be Topias. The NIPT test already told us in the early pregnancy that this little one would be a boy. I answer happily.

– Topias, a lovely name. The doctor says.

- We came up with the name years before, when a little boy with a blond hair ran past us in Suomenlinna, small island in cost of Helsinki, with a happy smile. The parents ran behind and shouted at little Topias to stop. At that moment, we decided that if we had a son, he would be Topias. I will tell the doctor about our experience.

Our infertility doctor continues: - Topias surviving the other twin miscarriage and uterine deformity is less likely than winning the lottery. In your case, this is neither luck nor coincidence, but the result of long-term, unyielding years of work.

- Of course, it was a coincidence that the embryo remained in this uterine deformity, where it could not be placed, for example, even the next attempt also. The nurse tells.

With a lump in my throat, I turn towards the screen and see a small person. Topias waves happily. I see him for the first time. Little dancing feet, a happy body and a hopeful wave. We'll meet again, I tell him silently. He is already close to me, after all, he has been a part of me for several months, even though I have tried mentally to keep him at a distance, when I have been afraid of losing the baby around the clock. In my heart, my child has been for much longer, my whole life, ever since childhood yard games.

The maternity clinic warns that in addition to feelings of happiness and wonderful anticipation, I can also experience conflicting feelings, such as fear, tension and low mood. However, I myself don't have time to experience happiness or low mood when I'm constantly stiff with fear and excitement. Every symptom, every feeling, every moment could be a sign of miscarriage. We've safely made it through the first quarter, but we're not quite halfway there yet. If only we could make it to the 25th week. My former colleague's relative's baby survived very well when he was born so early.

The day will come when we get to 4D ultrasound, which is a great new technology. I can really see you Topias, your face, your sweet nose and your little smile. Oh how sweet you are! My dear child, I will do anything to stroke your cheek. You are so close, yet so far. I see your smile, but it's out of reach. I'm sailing in the waves, smile as a lighthouse guiding me.

The last quarter starts.

– When is it safe to take Topias out by section? I'll ask many different doctors at the Women's Clinic.

- Now let's try to get Topias to stay inside as long as possible. This doctor also repeats.

The doctor doesn't understand enough how terrified I am. However, he sees through my determination, and I am unexpectedly directed to the fear group of expectant mothers. I'm sitting in the floor of one of the rooms of Women's Clinic with about ten others. Everyone else is afraid of childbirth except me. I've been directed here because I'm scared to death of losing Topias while I carry. I feel like I am the only different coloured ball in a ball pit. It feels like I'm being jumped on and I'm pressed to the edge. I can only tell the truth about why I'm here: I want Topias out right now, now that he's still breathing and doing well. I don't dare to tell others that otherwise my body will kill this child too. However, no one would realize the situation and think I'm crazy, so I keep quiet. We go to lie down, and I learned that if you can't sleep, you can gather a lot of strength even by lying down for a quarter of an hour. I also hear that someone had worked out after giving birth to get in better shape than before giving birth and their married life had brightened up a lot. We are told that when someone in the group is afraid of loosening up. I sigh. Everyone has different fears. I'm just afraid of my baby dying. It doesn't matter how much I tear, will it be from the South Pole to the North Pole, I don't care. If only I could stroke your cheek and make you smile from happiness.

During pregnancy, my mind is filled with worry. Expecting, as the name suggests, expecting and waiting, minute by minute, hour by hour, day by day, I'm just waiting for the time to fill up before my body ends this hope prematurely. I dare not do anything so as not to cause a miscarriage. I feel constant fear. Every movement of the baby causes fear about whether everything is okay, as well as if he does not move. Consultation visits are not happy pregnancy progress monitoring visits. Every examination is a threat of negative news that something bad has happened to the baby. Our life stops. We don't dare to prepare for the postpartum period. We're just waiting.

It's a cold afternoon at the beginning of the year. in the cold wind, I wobble from work again towards the hospital, which fortunately is located right next to my workplace. I have already visited the Women's Clinic many times, but I have always been turned away. Now there is no more than a month until the birth. As a first timer, I don't know what feeling is normal and what isn't. I can't stay still, so after the work I follow the snowplough across the road to the hospital area. Many cars are parked in the yard of the Women's Clinic. I climb the hospital ramp. Somehow, a strange feeling forces me to stop and pant in the middle of the hill before I get to the glass door. In the lobby of the women's clinic, I see a couple putting a newborn in a safety cradle. Only a small nose can be seen from inside the overalls. I turn to face the warden and his questioning look is in front of me again. I explain that I have come to be checked again. He kindly points towards the receptionists, whose attitude towards me exudes prejudice. I can't help but hear the "Here she comes again" comment. The other acknowledges the shared frustration with a nod. Of course, no one can know my background and the reality of my fears, there are so many patients. Still, I would hope that every patient would be received with the understanding that nobody wants to come to the hospital for nothing.

Kindly but firmly I state to the receptionists that I will sit in the lobby until they agree to have an ultrasound again, to ensure that nothing is wrong. Fed up looks. I don't care, I just say: - I'll wait until the morning, until someone looks. The nurse calls the doctor:

- Here is again the patient who is afraid for her child. The nurse looks at me and says: - Well, let's see then, go through those glass doors on the right again. You know the route.

The doctor places the ultrasound on my stomach. As his brows narrow, horror catches my breath.

- Labor must be started immediately. The doctor tells everyone.

- Here is a wheelchair. The nurse says as she comes through the door.
- All the amniotic fluid is almost gone. The doctor continues his speech. It later turns out that the placenta malfunction causes the amniotic fluid to be absorbed into my body instead of the amniotic fluid coming out. How was this not known and how had this not been prepared for? It's busy now. Topias doesn't have much amniotic fluid and I get a medicine to start labor. After severe contractions, sensors are installed on Topias' head and the battle for survival, which lasts almost two days, begins. I call Petri at work. He gets to say the words that he didn't think he would get to say to his co-workers for a long time: - I'm going to the maternity hospital now, we're having a child!
- Good luck! Colleagues' cheers.

Expected moment

I strongly declare that I want the most experienced and knowledgeable doctor available. I've heard that it could be ensured if you agreed to take a doctor who guides the students. This means that I lie in a semi-sitting position on the bed with my legs spread while ten students line up in a half circle formation in front of me. They are like a line of detectives or scientists peering over the shoulder of an experienced supervising doctor when he lifts the sheet and injects the anaesthetic: - Now I'm going to do an episiotomy so that Topias can fit out better.
- I haven't heard about it before, but in this situation I'm ready for any operation when Topias is in danger, do whatever is needed. I answer the doctor.
- This can be painful for a long time, but you will get through it. An experienced doctor encourages.

I would suffer from having my perineum cut for months. Everyone's eyes are watching my bottom end.

- It's good that now at least several pairs of eyes make sure that things go according to the textbook. I laugh.

Suddenly, the doctor turns to Petri: - Do you know that your wife's persistence and resourcefulness saved this child's life. If the loss of amniotic fluid had not been noticed, Topias would not have survived. Petri squeezes my hand and says: - Thank you.

- We have fought together to get here. I'll continue. It has been just as important for Petri as it has been for me that ultrasounds have been taken frequently.

One of the students comes along to the birth. He is a young friendly man studying to be a doctor. This would be his first birth as well. All three of us are nervous. Fortunately, an experienced and professional midwife guides us on how to get through this together. The midwife instructs the medical student and Petri to position themselves on both sides to support the legs while I push. All three of us work as instructed under the guidance of a professional. I will feel safe when the birth is approaching. Everything is still fine with Topias and now we would finally get him out. Right now, I can't be afraid anymore, I focus all my strength on surviving the painful contractions. If only everyone in the world had a safe and clean place to give birth to their children. Every parent and child in the world are equally valuable.

The epidural anaesthesia comes at just the right time and therefore pushing Topias out is almost painless. it takes all my strength, although luckily the pain doesn't confuse the situation.

Topias is crying! Finally! It makes us all cry out loud: Petri, me and the medical student. The midwife lifts the lovely little red-faced baby under my shirt to warm up. Topias, your lovely little head rests against my neck. I finally got you in my arms. Of course, you can't see a smile because of the crying, but I'll stroke your cheek. I know that I will do everything in my power to make your life full of smiles and happy moments, my dear child. My love is like a poem:

Before you were,
I wanted you
Before you were born,
I loved you.
Before you had been here even an hour,
I was ready to die for you.[6]

Petri looks at my pale greyish face. I have almost nothing left of my strength and Petri holds Topias in his arms. The nurses cannot understand how far we have come. We are treated like those who experienced a normal conception and pregnancy. However, we are not only talking about postpartum fatigue and the exhaustion of pregnancy, but about the powerlessness and traumas of the blows caused by years of battles and losses. They have no idea how exhausted I really am in the midst of this happiness. Even when I try to explain I don't get them to understand.

- It is our custom that the baby is in the care of its mother all the time. The nurse says firmly.

The evening is fast approaching, and Petri can't stay in the hospital because all the Family Rooms are booked.

- How would I survive the night with Topias? There is no way I can stay awake. I'm dizzy. I'm so exhausted I'm barely conscious. If I don't get help, the baby and I will soon be in full-time care somewhere else. I explain in desperation. The midwife on duty hears the seriousness of the situation in my voice and says:

- We can watch over Topias this night so that you can finally sleep for a while.

Everyone who has followed our long and rocky journey is happy to hear about Topias. Everyone wanted to see him right away. I don't really have the strength to rejoice with others when the exhaustion of the years erupts violently while I tried to breastfeed Topias. I try to at least smile a little at the visitors. The pursuit of happiness has taken all my strength, I don't have energy to be happy, I just am. In addition to fatigue, I am also worried about Topias' upcoming medical examination. I'm afraid that something serious could still be found. If only everything would be fine, and we would both be able to go home soon to sleep in Petri's care.

On the fifth day, Topias's check-up is at the hospital. The health check-up is performed by the doctor who supervised the birth with the team of candidates. He advises the students how to perform the inspection and what issues should be considered. Suddenly, Topias changes, as if drawing vertically, on one side to burgundy and on the other side to white. All the students rush closer to see this great wonder.

- I've only seen this a few times in my entire career! The doctor is happy. Nobody remembers to tell me what it's about.

- Not again! I don't want anything to happen to my child. What is it about?! I shout, but my voice is drowned in the noise of their conversation.

Medical terms follow each other in the middle of a huge buzzing. I do not understand anything. I start to feel dizzy again and I eventually fall to the floor. The doctor notices the situation and starts to calm me down while the students eagerly take care of Topias: - It's okay, this will pass soon. The harlequin phenomenon is harmless and has not been linked to any illness, Topias is fine, a strong and healthy boy. I look gratefully and even more exhausted at the doctor. Topias gets the little clothes on. I start pushing the wheeled baby bed towards our room. Now we can go home.

Petri comes to pick us up and carries his newborn son in the car's safety seat to the lobby. It's finally our turn to walk out of here happy and relieved. I never thought this day would come. Topias was born on Runeberg 's day. Johan Ludvig Runeberg is considered Finland's national poet, and he was also a teacher, journalist, priest and professor. What does life have to offer for our Topias? The Finnish flags were flying on Topias' birthday outside in the halls, and we are finally a family. As we walked towards the doors, I wondered if the Finnish saying "talks like Runeberg" applies to this child. It means that person is talking fluently, eloquently or loftily. I will later find that this is true. To our delight, Topias talks a lot even though he is very small. The guy is good with words and always have something to say. Having just started elementary school, he confidently states when the teacher asks about professions that his father is a bank mouse!

I stroke the cheek of Topias, my little baby. He has a contented look and seems to smile when touched. Finally, after so many years of waiting, we see your smile. You are finally here. Your smile is no longer just on the screen of the ultrasound machine, far away, out of reach, but it is real, tangible. Our lovely little boy. Now we can go home. I'm just about to push open the front door of the hospital when the door opens. My sister looks at us with a smile. She was coming to see Topias. Accompanied by a happy chatter, we walk out together. Sun shines. We descend with light steps down the same ramp, which I had climbed up with heavy steps many times in order to get to this moment.

At home, I sit happily on the top of swimming ring, Topias in my lap, but my bottom is completely torn. I don't know yet that I would sit there for a month and a half. It does not matter! Life is just the best! Although my breasts are bleeding, we will get through that too. The most important thing is that my child is well! He is growing and is happy with the formula, when I only get a third of the required amount of milk and that too is results of painful pumping. I don't worry about breastfeeding, because every parent is the best for their child in their own way. Love, closeness and taking care of basic needs are enough. I love my child more than anything.

As new parents, we receive well-intentioned advice and instructions for children's everyday life from our loved ones. As a result of years of trying, we have learned to filter out the views of others and trust our own instincts. New parents often panic when, for example, breastfeeding is made a big deal in conversations, as if it has to be successful. Even in substitutes, the children will grow up happy when you do your best as a parent. Coping of the parents is in the child's interest, even if a substitute is used to get baby to calm down and parents' sleep require it. Sometimes in dental care, you are asked to quickly put away the pacifier. I conclude that the best thing is that everyone in family can sleep. Let's keep the pacifier with us, even it would be only during the falling asleep phase. Individual support for families should be the starting point in everything. No family or situation is the same. Busy family life with a baby and children can tax a relationship if common sense is not used. Every family is perfectly fine and good enough as it is. A helping hand and a listening ear from those close to you are better than a pointing finger and a judgmental look. No one should be pushed to the end.

Every parent can do as they see fit, as long as the child and parents are fine. For us, this helped us survive in the middle of staying up all nights. I just wish that all parents could get to know their baby without the pressure of the environment, happily and calmly. We take Topias everywhere, even to a restaurant, when I can eventually go to one myself. I finally understand why children always go with their parents: we want to go everywhere together, after all, we are a family. At the same time, we worry about how others are doing. Remembering how difficult it was for us to see families with children before. Many are currently undergoing infertility treatments and may be looking at us with the same sadness. We try to take care of Topias in the stroller without being noticed and only express our joy to each other at home. We don't want others to suffer. I now understand how difficult it is to see other people's lives blinded by one's own experience.

It's evening and the reflux shift starts again. Topias vomits milk, not by gurgling but by vomiting in a curve. We take turns with my parents to watch over Topias. My Mother takes first sift early evening while I sleep, Petri continues after. I will stay up the whole night and my father will take over at 5am so I can sleep a bit before going to work. No need to explain anything to my parents, no blood, no mess or anything else. In this situation, I don't have energy to do anything else besides taking care of Topias and sleeping.

Next week at the counselling session, I will be asked what hobbies I have. I will tell them that I signed up for baby swimming and music lessons with Topias. The nurse at the clinic asks again: - No, what do you do?

I realize I have been doing nothing but taking care of Topias. I haven't had the energy for anything else. I'll think about it. I later hear that boxing is the best of all sports for treating a pelvis that has suffered during childbirth. To boxing, me! There is no end to the laughter. However, I am taking up boxing to get my hips in shape. After rushing to the first class in a hurry, I wonder how hard the training is, then I get hit in the face so that my lip is swollen and bloody. I've been beaten up by life before, but not this concretely! Well, it doesn't matter, as long as the hip gets in shape. At home, I complain to Petri that the boxing was otherwise nice, but the kicks were difficult, and I got hurt. Petri enlightens me by telling me that there is no kicking in fitness boxing. I check the class description online and realize that I was in the wrong group: it was an advanced group for kickboxing. Again, I got a good laugh by laughing at myself. The following week, I will go to training less hastily and find both, the right group and new strength in myself, physical and mental. I'd need them again.

Topias was born in the countryside, where we had moved with the inspiration of my goddaughter's family. You can hear sheeps nearby and the place is idyllic. During the spring, my strength returns, and I manage to do my thesis while Topias' naps and I graduate. I have finally finished my studies amidst work and infertility treatments, and I can fully focus on Topias.

When summer arrives, Topias should start crawling and then go on all fours, but with every crawl, one hand gets stuck under the belly. The hand is somehow damaged in a cramped birth. From the consultation, we are directed to physiotherapy. We train three times a day and eventually Topias starts crawling briskly. After that, he is crawling only for sort while, until he got up and learned how to walk before his 1st birthday and we have moved to Germany.

As a mother in new culture

Fate had intervened in our lives again, this time in a happy way. Petri gets the opportunity to go to work in one of the big centres of the banking world, Frankfurt. The decision to leave is a big one: Petri would work in the German language. Sure, he had studied German in middle school and high school, but he has never even been to a German-speaking country. Free time during the summer before the move is spent revising German grammar and vocabulary. The employer also promises to arrange private tuition for both of us on the spot, after we settle in Germany. Driven by the enthusiasm of youth and financial necessity, we quickly decide to move abroad. We have dreamed of living abroad at some point, and that opportunity came now. In addition to the burden of considerable debt that infertility treatments have piled on our backs, future adoptions would not be free either. Living in Germany is more affordable and with Petri's salary I could be at home with Topias longer. The chance to live abroad is also a wonderful opportunity to learn and experience a lot of new things.

For the first time, we would go on a journey together as a family towards the unknown. We already know that this will not be our last trip, because we still dream to get a little sister for Topias through adoption. We boldly sell our home and go on a journey. We do not know anything about everyday life in Germany, so the departure is of course exciting. Our whole life is packed into a moving truck. I load a huge amount of baby food on board for Topias so that everyday life will continue as usual until we settle down and find everything we need in Germany.

The ship takes us to Tallinn, Estonia and another ship to Germany and we will drive the highway towards Frankfurt. Beautiful landscapes and castles follow each other as we drive towards our new home. It is late evening and already dark when we arrive in the Frankfurt area. Petri reasons that we can find our way there ourselves if we just drive around looking for signs. We don't need a map and we don't have a navigator yet. Just like on the wedding night, we drive around again until we find our destination. I'm already ready to stop and ask for help in my weak German. Finally, Petri agrees to stop and slows down to a truck park on the side of the highway. I am with Topias in the darkness of the back seat. A group of lightly dressed women immediately come towards Petri's opened window to offer their services. Petri apologizes and politely refuses. We continue our journey. No route help was found at this stop.

Eventually, the landscape begins to change to mountains, and we come to the main street of the beautiful Königstein village. This would be our home street for the next few years. We have been to Frankfurt a couple of months earlier to tour vacant apartments with a consultant who mediates expat services. The detached house in the mountain village is admittedly at the high end of our budget, but we feel we deserve a little luxury after everything that has happened. We would get a small and safe base of our new home for our family to live our life. It would be good place for our loved ones to visit us too.

The view from the yard of our home down to the valley and again to the heights is beautiful. The street is quiet and with Topias we admire our neighbours' horses walking freely in the field. My shape is increasing rapidly, because the roads that start in front of our house are so steep that going to the convenience store with Topias in a stroller is a real daily workout.

Petri's workdays are long and train travels to Frankfurt and back is adding into it. As a housewife, integrating into Germany is difficult for me. I feel like I am on a long journey all the time, as I mostly take care of Topias alone during the day. I try to get involved in German everyday life and go to the village with Topias to take care of things. We arrive at the post office but in order to get in I have to climb a long set of outside stairs. I'm trying to ask in German and English if someone could help me with the stroller. No one helps. I finally manage to drag the stroller up. Sweat runs down my face as I go to the queue with outgoing letters addressed to "Finland". People look at me suspiciously, I'm not familiar in the village and I still speak German poorly. I wonder about the attitude, although I try to be friendly and Topias smiles at everyone. When it's my turn to go to the counter, the clerk takes the letters and reads out loud to everyone: - Finland, aus Finnland! So you are from Finland!

- Yes. I answer with a cautious nod.

All the people from the post office suddenly come to us and start admiring Topias. A woman in her fifties crouches down in front of Topias and exclaims: - He has such beautiful big blue eyes! I wonder in my mind why Topias' eyes are now suddenly wonderfully big and blue and why wasn't this the case five minutes ago? People help us out in large numbers to carry Topias and strollers and warmly welcome us to live in the village. Why did the fact that I was from Finland change people's attitude? Did they first think we were from somewhere else and why would that make people not want to get to know us? This possible disparity of values continues to bother me, it is completely against my own world of values. After that, without realizing it, I am suspicious of the new Germans I meet for a while, until I realize that I am acting just like them - suspiciously. I change my behaviour to be kind and open-minded towards everyone. Later, after ten years, when we return to visit Germany, I notice that the atmosphere of attitude has changed. Königstein has become modern and multicultural. It's wonderful to participate in the village's festivities, where people from different cultures dance in a procession through the village.

When Topias was a baby, Petri's colleague in Germany advised me to join a Finnish church. From the parent-child music club, we get friends to spend time with. I also get to be a teacher at the Finnish-school one day a week, and Topias gets to play with my friend's children at school. It's a nice change for both of us. Little by little, I learned from others how to live better everyday life in Germany. Only a few people in our village still speak English, so my German is improving with persistent effort every day. However, in Germany, there are so many unwritten ways of doing things that I often do something that others think is crazy. For example, I take the wrong colour garbage bag to the side of the road and have to try again after I finally realized what I should have done. I think that briskly head up and towards new disappointments.

Sometimes on the weekends, we get our relatives and friends visiting us from Finland, who we go together to explore Germany and neighbouring countries. It's nice that Germany is so close to everything. On weekends, you can conveniently drive to France,

Switzerland and many other places by car. In Germany, the wonderful Christmas markets are particularly memorable. Everything is so close in Central Europe. Petri enjoys Germany's wonderful castles and ruins and makes a lot of historical trips with visiting relatives and friends. In restaurants, we have a selection of kitchen utensils, whisks, ladles and other things to work with, so that Topias has something to explore while we eat. His own toys are too familiar to keep him busy while we eat. Fortunately, German's love children and children are allowed to run around in restaurants without being perceived as a disturbance. Especially the Greek restaurant in our own village becomes an important place for us when the friendly owners play with Topias. Me and Topias only participate in some trips with our loved ones coming to Germany. For example, Champagne and the battle locations of the Normandy landings are not for Topias. Those times we stay at home alone to dance to the rhythm of popular kids music. Topias is a lively child and on the busy streets of Germany we keep him in a "Loved baby" harness. He is a brisk walker and likes to be busy, so we often go to many outdoor playgrounds for children. They are brilliantly designed in Germany, and you can easily spend the whole day there. The park is like a large, green, natural amusement park designed for children of different ages, where you can sit on the grass for a picnic between the devices, feed the free-roaming animals and enjoy the beautiful streams and miniature alpine huts.

While we are in Germany, Finland wins the Eurovision Song Contest with Lord's Hard Rock Hallelujah song, which Topias too dances in diapers in front of the TV. I feel proud to be Finnish, but even more I rejoice in the unity of nations, when people from different countries celebrate together. At the same time, I feel homesick for Finland.

Afterwards, I feel like I can't describe the environment much, because my eyes have been all the time on Topias and his safety. I myself could not enjoy the scenery like others. My fear that something will happen to Topias keeps my eyes fixed on the child. I cannot lose him. One day when we are alone at home, I give Topias a small piece of strawberry. It catches in his throat. Frightened I start beating the boy on the back. It doesn't help and the colour of Topias' face starts to turn bluish. I quickly lift him into the children's Heimlich grip and bang him with all my might. The strawberry flies like a cannon to the floor and Topias starts to cry. I hold him in my arms and cry myself too. I have never been so alone as during those seconds when Topias could not breathe. I'm starting to miss Finland and my loved ones there more and more. My father has always hoped that my sister and I would build houses in our childhood backyard one day. Now that idea no longer seems like a crazy idea, but right and safe.

After a year, homesickness starts to weigh on me. My grandfather's illness brings the limitations of life in front of me strongly. I want grandparents and other loved ones to be involved in Topias' life. The job offer I received from Finland makes it financially possible for our family to return home. Petri, on the other hand, has a hard time announcing the need to terminate the expat contract and return to Finland after just one year. Fortunately, we get understanding from the employer again and the search for Petri's successor begins. He agrees to continue in Germany until a successor can be recruited. In reality, this means that Petri will live alone in Germany for six months. His evenings are spent flipping through books because e-books and streaming services are not yet available.

After returning to Finland, I will move with Topias to my parents and start working. Fortunately, the familiar work team that moved to the new organization welcomes me with open arms. I would have liked to be at home with Topias longer, but starting work is necessary due to the costs of the future adoption. It is hard for me to take Topias to kindergarten. I am constantly afraid that something will happen to our son and I will lose him. Topias is afraid of loud noises and one day the daycare calls that Topias has run from a church to the highway when the chruchs' organ starts playing. The nurse's quick action saves Topias from being hit by a car at the last moment. Even though he is safe and alive, the fear of losing him starts to creep into me again. Fortunately, my grandfather, other words called 'paappa' will live many more happy years with Topias. On his deathbed, he takes Topias' hand and says: - You are a good boy.

I strongly feel how the good words and deeds of everyone who leaves here continue to live in the hearts of those who stay here. I also cherish many good deeds of my grandmother, my friends and also my grandfather did and I want my children to remember, hear and learn from them. We live a normal everyday life. One day, Topias cheerly brings me a super small hand towel in the shower so I can dry my long hair with it. I thank his kindness with a smile, it's great that he tries to help. Every smile and good deed in everyday life, as well as every resolved cry and defiance, attach my heart more and more closely to Topias. In the wave of a family with children, we grow together, and I am happy.

As soon as Topias started to grow up and realize that his friends are getting little siblings, he too starts hoping for a sibling. We hope the same. We tell him that we have submitted an adoption application and one day we would receive a letter with a photo of Topias' sister or brother. However, that would still take years. Topias decides that until then our dog Iita is his little sister.

We thought about our living arrangements and decided to build our own home on a plot of land that belong to my parents. The planning of the house would be done following spring and building would start on the summer. We would continue to keep living with my parents, where we would have two bedrooms, bath and short distance to construction site. We are planning extra room on our new house for children we hope to have in future.

I I

The one who has born to be a mother,
she is the mother of all children,
and all the children of the world
she has pressed against her chest,
and the cry of the children of the world
in her ears she has begun to hear
for the children of the world speak
through the mouths of her own children.[7]

This proem has been my biggest strength during my infertility. Now when I am finally a mother, I want to be one for more children too. There are millions of children who doesn't have a family or a mother. I wish I could be a mother for some of these children.

A Ticket to Africa

I'm waking up. I'm not in the ambulance anymore, I'm being prepared for a procedure. I look into my father's worried, shocked eyes at the end of my bed. My positive father rarely has that look. I've seen it before, when I was young when I got into a car accident and in other serious situations that happened to loved ones. I had time to think about my childhood family for a while until I fall asleep, and in my dream, I return to my childhood home again, now as an adult.

The causes of my infertility were never fully understood, and my body still hasn't fully recovered from childbirth. Due to the established childlessness, the possibility of adoption opens up for us. I will start clarifying and preparing the matter as soon as I return to Finland so that we can start when Petri returns from Germany.

Adoption. The action of legally taking another's child and bringing it up as one's own. It is a legal procedure by which a new a parent-child relationship, is formed between the adoptive parents and the person to be adopted. The Save the Children organization describes that adoption is a rich life-long journey. That's what we're going for now.

Adoption is not charity. A child is not adopted to help, but the child has the right to come into the family as an expected and desired child. According to the Save the Children association, which is offering international adoption services in Finland, it is important in international adoption that the children get to thoroughly trained families that are well prepared to receive the child and support them in different stages of their life. We contact the organization and start adoption training and adoption counselling. We know it's a long and emotionally taxing process. Ten years later, having experienced a lot with my child, I understand that everything that went through in adoption counselling and coaching was necessary.

Waiting for an adopted child begins with queuing for counselling, which we wait for almost a year. The relief is great when we finally get to start counselling. Things are progressing and we are getting more and more convinced that adoption is the right step in building the family we dream of. Adoption counselling includes conversations with a social worker and a few training events where we hear the experiences of young adults who were adopted to Finland as children and do various group exercises. After a one-year counselling period, the long-awaited decision on permission for foreign adoption finally falls through our mailbox. We get to start the actual waiting.

During the consultation, we got to know different options and finally, inspired by my colleague's child, we end up adopting our next family member from Thailand. The waiting time is about a year. The year passes quickly in the happy intoxication of waiting and Topias is happy about the future sibling. After a year, we are told that the wait will get longer and last at least two years. After next year, we are advised to prepare for a three-year wait. The adoption process in Thailand is completely blocked.

Topias happily blows out one more candle from his birthday cake. I tell him that we are going to celebrate a few more birthdays before the little sister or little brother would join the party. We are still in Thailand's adoption queue. Although time passes, the adoption queue slows down even more. The worry is growing for us and other waiting families. The situation of international adoptions is starting to overheat in Finland.

During the long wait, we reflected that we hadn't realized how much emotion, pain and fear we experienced before adoptive parenthood. And all of this happens before we've even gotten to the search trip. At one time, we thought that the child would come to us as long as we were in contact with the adoption organization and took care of the paperwork. Since we have infertility as ballast, the situation is quite different. Adoptive parents go through tough training to earn parenthood.

For the adoption process, we need to send pictures of our home and the children's room to the adoption agency. We are currently building a house for ourselves, and during the construction we live with my parents. We prepare the home in my parents' upstairs and take beautiful photos, decorate like influencers for Instagram. What if we hadn't been able to cope with all the interviews and stages, when grief and longing for the child took away the strength at the same time? I don't even dare to think about that. You have to learn how to cope and pretend to be strong. There is no opportunity or courage to even ask what will happen if we can't make it. Will we lose the most important thing, the child, or at will the process be delayed again? Instead of harsh further investigation under magnifying glass, friendly and safe support and help would be needed in this matter as well. The staff of adoption organizations are friendly, but one's coping skills could be misinterpreted.

- You can't handle it? How are you going to cope with the child then? One could ask this. I dread these questions. The solution to coping would be to get the child home as soon as possible. I could handle the process and waiting better if things just went faster. Afterwards, we realize that each step was a necessary part of our growth as an adoptive parent. If only you could or dared to talk more about the limits of your own strength.

I remember a blog post I once read. If we thought that everything is just life, we wouldn't be in such a hurry to rush to recovery or hide our current condition from others. All that hiding, what a waste of energy when it's scarce anyway. What if you don't put on the mask of getting by until you can return triumphantly to tell the story of survival. This is so true. However, we don't dare to talk about these feelings to anyone yet. You just have to make it, you can't get tired now.

The most brutal thing is freezing the life situation for the duration of the process. Our health, work, living conditions and everything are thoroughly investigated, and the information is reviewed at regular intervals. The destination country expects, for example, health information, a certificate of employment and a criminal record extract to be no more than one year old. What if something changes during the years, we are expecting our child? Our health is especially worrying. We are healthy, but what would the situation be like when the information about the child comes out. Even if a health problem would be with just one of us, it could bring down the whole process for both of us, as it had happened to one family. It's hard to imagine what it's like to put life on hold while waiting for adoption until you experience it. We don't need to change anything radically in our lives. It's somehow unnerving to feel that nothing is allowed to happen or that it could affect having a child or at least postpone the process for years again. Mentally, it feels like our lives are stuck in place until the authorities in Thailand tell us about the child.

The situation is particularly difficult for those who are expecting their first child. We had experienced this hopeless wait during infertility treatments, but luckily, we already have Topias and are able to live the everyday life as a family also during the adoption process.

While waiting for the adoption to proceed, we are building a house in my childhood home yard. The construction project has already lasted for a very long time. The house supplier has made big mistakes in the frame installation, which took months to correct. During the day we are at work, in the evenings and even at night our hands are full of work around the house. I've been grinding metal for concrete casting. Petri spends all free time with my father and his own father bricking interior walls, tiling floors and installing furniture. Topias also has to live in the middle of a house building project, just like I did when I was a child. It didn't bother me at the time and Topias seems happy too. So, despite our tiredness, everything is progressing well.

I am a workplace representative at the exhibition stand. I just changed my shoes to low heels, so I have energy to continue. It's nice to meet people and find solutions to their needs together. A man I don't know approaches the stand. He comes to me and tells me that he works for a Swedish IT training organization. In addition to training Swedes, their team does projects in developing countries by training IT skills. The training is conducted completely remotely using computers and mobile devices. Sounds interesting. I will tell him that I have previously worked with a similar organization. It turns out that it is indeed the same organization and that it is expanding its operations to Finland. Maybe we could work together.

Later, the man contacts me with the head of his organization. They inquire about my work situation. I am in a six-month project from my own employer, and the project would end soon for me. The director remembers that I told him that I would like to go to Africa to help sometime when I am over 50 years old. That is correct. He asks if I could come work for them now. I could do charity work at the same time. The offer is attractive. I call Petri and he encourages me to accept the job, knowing that it could be the job of my dreams. The organization's goal "Education for All" fully corresponds to my own world of values, everyone must have the right to education. With the help of online education and mobile learning, it is possible to offer education in Africa also in areas where travel to bigger cities is difficult. The flexibility of online and mobile learning also gives more people the opportunity to study. In very poor villages in the countryside, there would be an opportunity to jointly acquire a cell phone, to which instructions can be sent by text message, for example, on how to purify dirty water into cleaner drinking water in the heat of the sun. In this way, children's diarrhea can be significantly reduced in the villages. After considering the offer a short while, I accept the job.

My first business trip with my new employer is going to Ghana. After the workday, I ask about the possibility of visiting one of the children's homes in the area. Our local contact person will arrange the visit. Many happy children play together on the cement floors of the orphanage. I notice the children startle at my arrival. Maybe they think I'm taking one of them with me. I squat down and talk to two little girls. We don't have a common language, but through toys we can achieve a little play. I wish I could take the girls with me to Finland, we would have a place for them in our family. Of course, adoption doesn't work like this, but uniting the child and parents is the result of comprehensive expert consideration. However, I have a strong feeling about those two little Ghanaian girls that we could rethink the choice of country for adoption after the queues in Thailand have stopped completely. We could adopt from anywhere in the world. I call Petri. He agrees and says:

- An adopted kid is our child, regardless of where he/she comes from. When you return, lets' ask the adoption organization what the queues look like in different countries.

- Great. I rejoice.

Up until now, we have only had experience with a son adopted from Thailand, now we are expanding our horizons and already during my trip we will start to find out in more detail the criteria of the countries that we would be suitable for and with which Finland has an agreement.

On the way back, at Ghana's airport in the capital, Accra, the feeling of insecurity hits me for the first time. Everyone's suitcases are opened at the security check. As I prepare to open my own bag, the man in front of me suddenly digs out a bundle of bills and shakes the hand of the security inspector. Banknotes change hands. His bag will not be opened. What is he hiding there? I'm going on the same plane as a man and his bag. My bag is being opened. I swallow a couple of times and decide to get on the plane. Fortunately, nothing happens on the flight, and we arrive in Helsinki.

We hear the news that Finland has signed an agreement with Kenya on international adoptions and they are looking for first couples to join. There would be no queue. Petri points out with some doubt that there is no queue also because, according to Kenyan legislation, one would have to move to Kenya for the duration of the long monitoring and trial process. I would be ready to pack my bags right away, Petri, on the other hand, is researching about the security situation in Kenya from the websites of the Ministry of Foreign Affairs and the EU. Topias could not be taken anywhere. Petri is also thinking about leaving in terms of both of our jobs. It would not be possible for Petri to work from Africa, so I am discussing the matter with my own employer. What would he think if I went to Kenya for a longer period and would work there? He is positive about it, although the length of time spent in Kenya is unknown. It could be four months or even a year. On the other hand, things could certainly be progressed more smoothly if I were there.

I've taken care of the matter with my employer. Next, I need to talk around Petri: - Could you think that we would leave, even though all kinds of things are happening there? The situation is new even for Finland and uncertain for everyone?" In Petri's opinion, who thinks things through and plans, this is not the best possible sales pitch: - We haven't even finished building our house. We would need to move again. What about that security?

Petri's previous experience of Africa is only as a child from a few tourist trips in North Africa (as well as the Canary Islands, which Petri jokingly reminds are part of the African continent). Petri has no experience in that part of the world and so the idea of a change seems a bigger decision than moving to Germany. Although now we could do it with familiar English.

Staying in Kenya for several months turns out to be possible in the end when I have my job and Social Security is ready to pay Petri parental allowance for the period of stay in Kenya from the moment the child is handed over to our care. After the workday, Petri says that he thought about it a lot during the day, but the decision is so big he needs more time to ponder this over. That very same evening, Petri suddenly says: - We want a child, and we want it as soon as possible from anywhere in this planet, we're going to Kenya!

Petri is nervous, but he still wants us to contact the adoption organization in the morning. The trip allows Petri nine months of parental leave. Petri took a three-week paternity leave, when Topias was born, but this joint period with two children would be a completely different kind of memorable experience and opportunity. The whole time we have been together we have been goal-oriented and planning, even though we had to adapt to surprising big changes time after time again. We hadn't been able to imagine this stage in our lives either, but the more we think about it, the more it starts to feel right decision for us.

Little by little, things start to clear up as much as it is possible as our family moves towards the unknown. One family is already on the

71

ground as a pioneer and kindly shares information with interested families. The family has already gotten their adoptive son home at the point when we make the decision to move our application from the Thai adoption queue to the Kenyan queue. We hear more about the practical process in Kenya from the adoption organization. For the first three months, the social worker visits the family to monitor the adoption child's progress settling their new home, and after that the court proceedings would begin. You can go home with the child only after the legal process has been completed, which requires several hearings.

Now is the moment when Petri would have to tell the news to his employer again. Petri talks a little nervously about his intention to take a long parental leave in Africa. The employer is 100% supporting about it, and at the request of his colleagues, Petri promises to keep a blog about the progress of our trip, so that the adventure can also be followed at the workplace in Finland.

The Kenyan authorities require slightly different documents compared to those sent to Thailand. This time, updating the papers doesn't seem as heavy as the previous times and things are progressing again. For the papers to be sent to Kenya, we stand next to each other for a photo. The local culture center and its beautiful pool sparkle in the sunlight. Our faces look happy in the picture and our hearts are full of hope. It is certainly that, but most of all we are exhausted from the preparations, and we experience a constant fear of the insecurity of the upcoming trip, especially for Topias. However, his joy at the likely speeding up of the process drives us forward with excitement. Topias tells everyone that he will soon be a big brother. I really hope we could see a little photo of the child already. All we know for certainty is that child would be younger than Topias as the local law requires.

I'm going on a business trip to Kenya. It is exciting to visit our future homeland. My Kenyan colleague who lives in Finland is traveling with me. It is safe to go on a journey with him. We also visited his home in a smaller town outside of Nairobi. I want to absorb all the information about this country and the life of the people there that is possible in such a short trip. The trip is a memorable and great experience as we prepare for the upcoming move.

On the flight, we make a stopover in Dubai. Everything at the airport is brilliant. Instead of shopping, as we walked, I observed people. I notice a girl of African descent, maybe 12 years old. Surrounded by a group of men, she follows a rich-looking Arab man dressed in a long white suit who looks like he's from the Middle East. The girl's expression is sad. Her mother or other children are nowhere to be seen. Our eyes meet. It's like she wants to tell me something. I would like to go and ask how she is, is everything okay. I don't dare, though. Nothing can happen to me now; I can't put myself in danger for Topias and our child waiting for adoption. I thought about what I could do. At that time, I hadn't heard about flight attendants helping children who are traveling on possibly wrong grounds. I wondered if all the people around me were part of the same big machine and if there was anything that could be done. The clerks serve the men diligently. I might have to bring Topias through Dubai airport on our way to Kenya. The adoption process must not be jeopardized by any skirmishes, so I decide not to do anything. I still think about that girl repeatedly. Even then, as I put my head down at the airport, I decided that I would never again fail to open my mouth to find out by myself or with the help of others how people are doing. I want to help everyone and that's what I've been doing ever since.

On the flight, a 17-year-old youth wearing a neat suit sits next to me. He seems to be from somewhere in the Middle East. I ask him: – Where are you traveling? The young man says: - There in front of us in the second row of benches, the older man with dark features, dressed in a white, long suit, is my uncle. I am going to work in his factory for two years.

- I am also on a business trip. I manage to reply before he continues his story.

- I have known all my life that this would happen, it was already told to me as a child. Childhood ends here. I will miss my mom and my siblings.

I reflected in my mind that luckily, I have not been forced into anything, not when I was young, and not now. I am driven forward only by my own desire to be a mother. I listen to him throughout the flight and try to encourage him that the time will certainly pass quickly and that he will cope well with everything that comes his way. I try to be a mother or even a big sister to him for a while or just a person, someone who cares. We land and I wish him all the best. He smiles. I never see him again after that.

In Kenya, we visit several cities and villages to initiate cooperation, which would continue after we move to Kenya. At the last breakfast at the hotel, a strange, strangling feeling takes over my throat. I'm moving here, not to a hotel, but to live somewhere for an indefinite period. I will also bring my family here and get a new family member. How will everything turn out here and how it is going to be like to live here when you can't get out? Without our child we won't return. I take a deep breath. If only I had a photo of my future child, it would help cut off the wings of uncertainty. I think about all the good things that I have already encountered on my journey, the beautiful nature and friendly local people. There are many wonderful things to experience here for Topias too, as long as we take care of safety according to the instructions given by my colleagues, my experienced manager and others. I calm down and decide that the upcoming adoption journey will be a positive and memorable experience. It's good to be here, I decide to focus on everything positive.

Through the storm

We prepare for the adventure of a lifetime with enthusiasm and excitement. The UN mentioned Nairobi as one of the most unsafe cities in the world already in 2001. We don't let this information scare us, instead we focus on planning how we can minimize security risks as well as possible. Knowledge drives us to equip ourselves: water purification tablets and baby carry-on backpacks to hold the children on our backs, money for shoes if everything else has been robbed. We couldn't even imagine how ruthless the looters are and what kind of fierce climate change is hitting us at this stage. Least of all, we couldn't have imagine how much the threats of this this journey are directed at the most important things: the life, health and safety of our children and the child's right to be in our family.

Kenya gained it's independence from British colonial rule in 1963. For twenty years, a one-party system prevailed in the country, although relations between tribes have always been more important than party lines. In total, there are 42 tribes in Kenya, half of which have less than 100,000 people. Tribe is more important to most people than nationality. Like many African countries, Kenya's population growth is one of the biggest development challenges: a nation of more than 50 million people grows by one million a year. More than 70% of the population is under 30 years old. In bit over ten years since our visit, the population has grown by almost a 30%.

When we leave to Kenya, we don't have too much knowledge of the country except that it is located on the equator and it is likely to be hot there. Despite its location on the equator, Kenya is not rainforest region. There are two rainy seasons in the year, the "long rains" in the spring and the "short rains" at the end of the year. Nairobi is located at an altitude of more than one and a half kilometres and the temperature does not seem to be as high as we had feared. The annual average temperature is below the Finnish temperature limit. Nairobi's name comes from the Masai- tribes' word for "cool waters".

In our home at Espoo, we prepare for the trip well ahead, even if we don't know when we're leaving. I study information about animals with Topias and Petri rationally studies travel information. We also test the equipment we have purchased. Topias sits in the children's carrier and we fasten him with the belts. Topias laughs as Petri lifts the ring on his back and walks along the living room. Topias is happy because he can see well from high up. I'll arrange a smaller baby carrier: - Your little sibling will come here; you can have toys or snacks in here too.

- Yes, juice. The answer comes from the other backpack.

Petri is growing as a person all the time at a fast pace, the closer the departure gets. He really needs to go into the unknown for the first time. Petri tries to gather all information he can get to control his fears. Even if he wants to, he won't have all the necessary information. Courage takes more and more space from planning.

On one working day, the office is quiet. The sea behind the window is beautiful, even though the winter ice covers its surface. The call interrupts our concentrated tapping of computers. The caller is an adoption from the organization. I'll shoot up from my chair.

- A little girl is waiting for you in Kenya. A friendly female voice tells.

- Can we get a photo of her? I'll ask her.

- Yes, I will send you all the information now. She will answer.

My heart skips a beat with happiness and all my senses are activated to work in overdrive. My co-worker and I are hugging. She will later become my little daughter's Godmother. It's finally happening. The whole family will move to Africa.

I'll call Petri right away and open an email at the same time. The adoption officer promised to send Melissa's picture encrypted. Melissa. We have decided to give her that name if the child is a girl. Her current name would become her second name. I wanted a beautiful name for her that would be easy to pronounce in different languages. Unlike my name Päivi, which always makes traveling challenging. I asked my Kenyan colleague how he feels about the name Melissa, would it be good in Kenya as well. He says the name means "fancy" in Kenya. So it is a good name.

I am very happy. The picture opens and there you are, a little girl in a sandbox. I look at your picture for a long time, you are like a fairy. You are smiling thoughtfully in the picture. What are you thinking my little girl? I wish I could already be with you and smile with you! Even now your smile is unattainable. Petri and I rush to the adoption office so we can get things started right away.

Suddenly, the wait is only a few weeks. We get the necessary goods. We have only had 6 months' time to live in our recently completed house and have been finishing the last construction work at the same time. Petri is finishing the sauna in a hurry, so that we have time to take at least one soak in our own sauna before we leave.

We get all the necessary vaccinations. We promise Topias a Lego package, if he also promptly drinks the terrible cholera vaccine. Two big glasses quickly go into the little boy's mouth, and we head to the toy store.

We send the passports to Stockholm for the visa. We celebrate Christmas and New Year with Topias and our relatives. We gather in the living room everything we think we might need in the next half year. We cram as much stuff into our suitcases as we can carry. On intercontinental flights, each person would be allowed to carry only two suitcases, but we realized this after redeeming a separate flight to

Nairobi trough London. Topias packs his most important belongings, eight kilos of metallic Cars-movie figures in his small bag. On the last evening, we go to our own sauna for the first time. In the morning we would fly via London to Nairobi to meet our daughter.

The year 2010 starts with snow and there is a blizzard in London. Petri has taken our suitcase to the airport the day before departure. We arrive at Helsinki-Vantaa airport on the day of departure to find that the British Airways flight from London has not arrived. Our flight has been cancelled and we must book seats on a new flight for the next day. We don't mind as we are so excited. Soon we would have the two children we had been hoping for a very long time. Life is finally moving again in the right direction, and we gain strength from it.

We arrive at the airport again the next day. Our hand luggage is illuminated and the clerk smiles when the contents of Topias' bag with the toy cars and scenes are revealed. Topias loves to act out different scenes from the movie. The bag has everything he wants to take with him, including his stuffed sleeping bunny. With these, Topias can feel at home anywhere in the world.

Topias sits happily in his seat on the plane, puts on his hearing protection and starts studying the safety instructions. The snowstorm has moved to Helsinki and our flight is considerably late. The flight goes well anyway and we land in London. We drag hand luggage from the plane. We don't have a direct connecting flight, so we have to collect our luggage and then check in again on the next flight to Nairobi. The change has been calculated carefully to avoid long airport waiting periods with a four-year-old son. When we get off the plane, Petri states that we are late for our connecting flight. We would need to spend the night in London.

We are waiting for suitcases from the hold, which never come. Due to the snowstorm, the bags have disappeared somewhere from us and hundreds of others. We report the bags as lost and hope to find them the next day when we continue to Nairobi. On the other hand, we don't really need our bags now since we're stuck in London. Shorts and summer dresses stuffed into bags are little use on the snowy streets of London. Petri arranges accommodation for us to stay at nearby, and in no time, we take a taxi to the hotel with our only suitcase that arrived in London. The hotel is large and clean, and the rooms are equipped for winter in the English style: thick curtains and a small heater placed on the table keep the room temperature just right. Fortunately, a warm bath warms Topias up before he slips under the covers.

Meanwhile Petri arranges a new flight for us. The next day's flight to Nairobi is full and we would have to stay at the airport hotel for another night. There will be additional costs for being late for the flight and transferring tickets. I am grateful for Petri's careful preparation: the insurance company reimburses the costs related to flights and accommodation in full and agrees to pay for other necessary purchases in addition: clothing suitable for the weather, hygiene equipment and a few toys for Topias to replace those lost with the luggage.

Petri has only visited London once before. At that time, he took the subway directly from the airport to the City for a meeting and back to the airport. This time either we won't be going sightseeing in our summer clothes, but we'll take the subway to Hamley's toy department store in city center. Topias is excited about the multistorey toy paradise. Sellers demonstrate toys by playing them. A child's joy and wonder make us parents, in higher mood as well. Both Topias and Petri are interested in double-decker buses and black taxis whizzing through the streets.

The next morning, we have already packed our stuff into a new suitcase and are heading to Heathrow's airport for flight to Nairobi.

Ahead would be a trip to Kenya for an indefinite period. Everything familiar and safe, as well as loved ones, are left behind. With Topias sound asleep next to me, I reflected on everything I had learned from Kenya on the flight to Nairobi, especially in terms of safety.

My future colleague in Kenya has said that the police department is very different there than in Finland. In Finland, my experience of the police at work is limited to a one moment before we left for Kenya. In the backyard of our newly built house, my parents' yard borders with a forest. From there, we saw unexpectedly blue lights late at night. I looked out the window and saw the police and alert drug dogs rummaging through my parents' compost. The police dogs stuck their muzzles under Topias's playhouse as well. I opened the door to ask if we could be of any help. Simultaneously Topias stuck his head out from behind me through the crack in the door. I wondered what really happened there. The police instructed us to stay inside. At the same moment, I saw a man on other side of the big lawn trying to run away from the police from the forest, through the yard and towards the road. The policemen ran and knocked him to the grass. The man was handcuffed and taken to the car. I explained to Topias that there is nothing to worry about, everything is fine. The police rang our doorbell. Our yard was used as a hiding place for drugs, since it is so peaceful, and we don't have a fence between the yard and the forest. You can move freely in the darkness between the forest and the road without being noticed. In Finland, you can always trust the police and the service is good. I hope we wouldn't have to deal with the police in Kenya other than for the necessary official adoption papers.

Adaption

Take care of yourself and those who suffer
Give alms to those who need it to live
Remember to build where the house falls to the ground
Try to encourage those who waver in their decisions
Because everyone who receives help,
someday realizes how to pass it on too [8]

I listen to this song every time it comes on the radio. Finnish singer/songwriter Pave Maijanen's lyrics resonate deeply in my feelings and values.

Unlike most people who embark on the adoption journey, I play two different roles. Firstly, I am here to get our new child home. Secondly, I am working with something that is most important to me. I am training and helping villages and communities to develop.

The plane lands and we look in wonder at the view from the window. Compared to Heathrow, the airport is small and downright barren. The suitcases roll into the green-walled arrival hall, where a cooling breeze blows through the openings in the ceiling. The adoption organization's minibus is waiting for us at the airport. Our suitcases arrive and we lift them into the car. During the long drive, we look at the scenery, Topias eagerly and Petri clearly still tense. Petri observes everything and tries to understand what he sees. Strange-looking trees lined the road. People are walking along the dusty, reddish roadside. There are a lot of them. The air is hot, but on the air-conditioned minibus we are like inside our own cooler little bubble. I wonder about how Petri will adapt here. Although there is no alternative options, we have to adapt.

The first moments in the adoption organization's car are spent making sure that Topias is all right and trying to remember landmarks and understand where we have come. In the end, the journey is not very different from arriving in any new place. The heart rate stabilizes, and we slowly start to adjust to the idea that for time being our life is here.

Nairobi is the capital of more than three million people. Kibera that is based in Nairobi is the second largest slum in Africa, in an area of less than three square kilometres, where officially lives two hundred thousand people but according to some estimates, it could be as many as one million people. In the UNESCO World Heritage Site of Suomenlinna (small island on coast of Helsinki) less than a thousand people live in an area of similar size. The population density of Helsinki, the capital of Finland, is just over three thousand inhabitants per square kilometre. In Kibera, the corresponding number is 80,000, but based on unofficial figures, it could be even 400,000. Although Kenya is suffering from population growth and population structure as well as the effects of climate change, it is a beautiful and exotic country at the same time. In its national parks, you can see elephants, lions, giraffes, zebras, flamingos and countless other species familiar from nature documentaries in their natural environment. A beach holiday is possible in Mombasa, in the south-eastern part of the country located on the Indian Ocean.

Tourism is the country's second most important source of income right after cultivation of coffee, tea and flowers. The cultivation of coffee and tea is becoming more difficult due to the drought caused by climate change. Kenya has long been a popular travel destination due to social stability and well-organized tourist services. In recent years, however, Kenya has also suffered among other things from the uncertainty caused by terrorism. Climate change can be seen in Kenya in the form of violent heavy rains, and in generally climate change is felt most strongly in developing countries. Drought is increasing in low-lying areas, and which especially affects girls and women whose job it is to fetch water. Shepherds produce up to 90% of the meat grown in East Africa. The increase in drought forces shepherd girls to marry urban men, because they have running water in their apartment. Increased drought, extreme temperatures and violent, shorter heavy rains than before are discouraging food production and at the same time straining society struggling with problems caused by population growth.

The country has a lot to develop, and China's influence can be seen, for example, in the modernization of the country's road infrastructure. Chinese engineers manage road construction sites, they wear traditional Asian triangular hats lined with foil to block the sun's heat. The shelves of our local market are full of affordable household goods and toys made in China. We find out that a knife worth one euro has the same quality in both Finland and Kenya. Apparently, there is a market in other parts of the world for goods that are obviously not suitable for Europe. At the same time, the country has already taken steps to introduce higher technology, such as for example the utilization of thermal heat in energy production.

There are two main languages in Kenya, English and Swahili, and in addition many languages spoken by different tribes. The violence caused by the fraud of the 2007 presidential election is fresh in our memory when we arrive in Nairobi, the capital of Kenya, in January 2010. Fortunately, the situation has calmed down and we do not experience threatening situations related to tribal disagreements during our time in Kenya.

Our minibus arrives to the home of another Finnish family who came earlier on the adoption trip. They had decided to live in a detached house in Nairobi. We are grateful to them and other adoptive families from different countries for the sense of community between families. Everyone is ready to help each other and share the good practices they have found, so that everyone's everyday life in the new country runs smoothly. Kenyans are also friendly and happy to give advice.

We spend a first couple of nights in a Finnish family's home and at the same time we are looking for our own place. It's nice that Topias gets a playmate right away and our journey is off to a successful start. I notice Petri's cautious, worried look as we slip under the mosquito net spread over the bed on the first night. We are prepared for malaria by taking antimalarial medication in advance, even though there is practically no risk of malaria on the height of Nairobi. We listen to the strange world of sounds from behind the fence surrounding the yard and fall asleep exhausted from the journey. The night watchman hired in the house watches over our sleep on the first night of our adoption trip in Africa.

In the light of day, the large yard of a detached house looks safe and sheltered. The night watchman has started a 60-kilometer bicycle ride back to his home village at dawn. At the breakfast table, while discussing adoption everyday life, we get our first experiences of everyday life. The process includes living with the adopted child, home visits by a social worker and a few court hearings. The rest of the time is just waiting and spending time with the family. Of course, I be working myself, so my own journey is different from the adoption journey of many others. In Kenya, the adoption process is long from the point of view of foreigners due to the fact that there is no distinction between domestic and international adoption.

The coordinator of the adoption organization has already searched for a few available apartments based on the search criteria and the rent that we have announced in advance. We are going to see three apartments in estates which accommodate adoptive families from different parts of the world. We had not thought that we would live in a detached house, but based on the first experiences, it seems like a good idea. However, In the end, we end up living in a fenced apartment building where several Finnish and European families on the adoption journey live. The yard is surrounded by high walls, on top there is an electrified barbed wire fence. Dark water slowly flows in a wide stream on one of the sides bordered by a metal fence. Armed guards are on duty at the gate. In Finland we were not used to security guards and guard dogs, but in Nairobi it is apparently necessary. The courtyard area has a swimming pool area and pleasant greenery. Not many locals seem to live in the apartment complex. It seems hard to think how big the difference in safety and living conditions are on the other side of the wall.

Our apartment is located on the first floor. It immediately looks like home, even though the windows have bars. When we enter, on the right is the kitchen and on its wall is the lizard that lives with us. Topias names the gecko "Gekkos". The apartment has three bedrooms and a bathroom down a long hallway. From the large bright living room there is access to the balcony protected by bars. In connection with the kitchen, there is a separate pantry equipped with wooden shelves the length of the whole wall. Behind the kitchen is a utility room for cleaning equipment and a washing machine. There is also a microwave on the wall, from which our first job is to evict a flock of cockroaches.

A large supermarket is a short walk or taxi ride away. At first, we dare to move only by taxi, but gradually we start walking. Topias is safely on Petri's back in a carrier with snacks and toys. I wish there would be a day already when I too have a backpack on my back and there is Topias's little sister. Petri wants to get to know the area well in daylight, because he wants to be familiar with the surroundings in case something surprising happens. In the first days, we go around a lot of nearby areas. While walking, we see Kenyans selling beautiful handicrafts. I will immediately buy a hand-woven basket for fruit in the kitchen. I thought that even with these small actions we can help. At least I want to believe I'm helping. Unfortunately, I later find out that helping a single person can be a bad idea in a heavily tribal culture.

It is clearly important for Petri to create a safe and functional everyday life amid a foreign environment. He would be here with the kids by himself when I left for work. Tap water is not drinkable, so Petri carries drinking water from the local market in 20 liter plastic bottles. The consumption of beverage bottles is high, so it is great to notice the bottle recycling operating in the shopping center. We also use bottled water for cooking. Petri has brought water purification equipment from Finland. We pour tap water from the bucket on the shelf in the utility room almost constantly, slowly through the filter into another bucket on the floor. We use this water to disinfect vegetables, fruits and vegetables. Before use, we wash them in a container of water, into which we drop a chlorine tablet. After processing, a light rinse with bottled water, after which they are ready for use. We want to avoid food-borne stomach diseases. This is how Petri begins to create a home for us in Africa.

Already in the first evenings, we get to use flashlights when power cuts start to occur. This is normal and you have to get used to it. Even after getting the internet, we notice that often it doesn't work. It's okay, as long as we get Melissa home.

We are animal lovers and enjoy being in nature. In Finland, you can leave home on foot, by bike or by car and experience nature freely. Lapland is incomparable, a real nature's amusement park, where we have screamed with excitement rafting, hiking and kayaking. In Kenya, nature experiences are also wonderful, but they must be planned well in advance to ensure safety. Fortunately, we quickly find places where you can breathe in the beauty of nature and experience the wonders of animals. Especially the giraffe park and the care park for orphaned baby elephants make us happy. Instead, the barren cages of the animal shelter for abandoned animals are shocking. We want to help as much as one family on this journey can.

It's early morning. We walk with Petri and Topias to a store further away for a change. There is a playground for Topias. There is no sidewalk, so we walk in line on the side of the road, there are a lot of cars and exhaust fumes. I notice a young mother crouching on the side of the road. She has a baby on her back and a little boy younger than Topias on the ground, drawing in the sand. Mother roasts corn on a small fire and sells it to people passing by who are hurrying to work. Several hours later we are returning from playground and the mother and children are still in the same place. I thought about children's lives in the middle of cars and exhaust fumes, in the sand and in the heat. How in still the child must be. I thought about a parent's constant concern for their children's lives, even the slightest accident and the child would be gone.

The sun rises and sets near the equator at almost identical times. For safety's sake, you must get home before sunset. The everyday life of the locals is challenging. Many people seem to be working around the clock during all daylight hours. Africans are friendly and would like it to show, but the conditions are so harsh in many places that there is no strength to smile. There are too many painful experiences.

I had received instructions from more experienced visitors to Africa that every day there should be only one thing that needs to be done. People come when they can and leave when they have to. When everyone is there, you go through the one thing that is most important. Everything on top of that is a plus and will be successful if things go well. This model was different from what I am used to in Finnish working life. Kenyans descriptively say that Europeans have clocks, but we Africans have time. We could certainly learn something from this. After returning to Finland, I intend to keep the main goal clear in meetings and projects, I will choose the most important thing that at least needs to be accomplished. The rest is added value. Our cooperation with the Africans has proven to be fruitful as both learn from each other. Combining different ways of working brings great results. The trip is also interesting from work perspective.

We sit in a restaurant and wait for food. It will come when on its own time. The waiting continues in agencies, the courthouse, the police station and at home while waiting for a social worker. We learned that it is necessity to have snacks for children. You always need have something to eat, drink and to play with. Waiting is only certain thing.

When my work pace is not so busy, I find myself constantly coming up with more things to do and trying to help people as best I can. It's hard to slow down. In Finland, we are used to rushing from work to dinner and the kid's football practice. Here we play and draw with Topias ourselves. It's great to observe small things with the child instead of frantically looking for a parking spot outside the soccer field. I feel like this trip makes us all happier. I decide that hobbies in Finland will be reduced and continued more on the children's terms. Little by little, I notice that after slowing down a bit, my health improves all the time, and I still can get the important things done. When there are not too many things to do in a day, concentration and quality improve. I cannot save the whole world in one go even if I wanted to. One thing at a time and working together, we can make changes for the better.

My colleague and I are going to visit a village. The purpose is to negotiate the launch of a cooperation project there. As usual, the day is sunny and hot. We stop in the center of the village for a drink. As we stand there, I notice a group of five children arrive. A seven-year-old girl briskly leads the group, the youngest is about two or three years old. All children walk barefoot. Suddenly, the children notice a big toe sandal abandoned by an adult on the side of the dirt road. Children rush to the sandal, and everyone would like it. They are waiting for the eldest child to decide who will get the old sandal. The girl decides that this time it's the youngest child's turn to get the sandal. I will never forget the look on the face of a small child when he walks past us dragging a large adult sandal. He is bursting with happiness and pride; his smile lights up the entire village. These are unforgettable moments of joy, of joy and justice.

In the evening I go to the market. A small, malnourished child comes to ask for money. At first, I'm unsure what to do and who might be watching me and the child. I decide to buy bananas and water for the child so that he can cope. I ask him to eat them in my presence. I will give a little more money so that he has something to take to those who may have told him to beg.

The next morning, me and my colleague walk to the slums of Kibera. Narrow alleys are lined with rows of shack apartments. Our local partner tells us that living in Kibera progresses in order: as apartments become available, everyone moves forward in the queue, until finally the opportunity to enter the apartment buildings built in the area becomes available. The system seems to be working.

There are also very large income differences in Kenya. On the other side of the road past the dusty tin houses of Kibera, a green, large park area opens, a private 18-hole golf course.

The people we meet in Kibera are friendly. They help each other and during the day there is no disorder anywhere. We go to our partner's home, which is built from sheet metal and fabrics. There, 12 people live in one room. The space is divided with a blanket into two parts, one side has an old sofa and the other side a sleeping area. Work is done in three shifts, so there is enough accommodation for everyone. During the day, everyone is outside. The residents offer me tea. I drink it gratefully, even though it feels wrong to take from the little they have. Fortunately, I can offer project work to our local partner, and he helps the community. My colleague tells me that in Kenya school uniform is extremely important for children who wander around without an adult. It tells others that they are expected at school, so it is not so easy to trick or kidnap the child anywhere. We will later organize school uniforms for all the children of a small slum school.

We continue our journey through the alleys of Kibera. We visit a small school and a craftsman's workshop, where I buy gifts. The handicrafts of Kenyans are great. Clay, metal, fabrics, magazines and other natural and waste materials get a new life in jewellery, dishes, decorative objects and clothes. Suddenly we notice a mother holding her child and a large group of people have gathered around her. We approach people. They say that the child has had a high fever for a long time. I notice that the child's tongue has already turned white. The mother cannot afford to take her child to the hospital. I ask if we could borrow a milk cart so that we can transport the child to a nearby hospital. I decide to pay for the hospital visit. About 10 euros is a small amount for us for a doctor's service. The child gets help and is saved at the last moment. Our partner says that he had malaria. My family and I had already taken malaria medicines when we came to Kenya, just to be safe. It is a negligible price for us to avoid a serious illness, while for the resident, the cost may be too great to save a life. The injustice of the world makes me angry again. I intend to help others as long as I shall live.

There is no properly functioning waste treatment system in the area, so a large common mountain of waste has been piled up at the end of the houses. We climb the mountain of waste. From there you can see the entire Kibera region, an endless unbroken blanket of tin roofs. I sit down. Everywhere is peaceful. I don't know why, but I want to sit on it for a longer time. It somehow feels like I've arrived. It feels like a genuine, non-pretending, communal atmosphere where people help each other, the kind of place I'd always like to be.

Plan International is a development and humanitarian organisation that promotes children's rights, is doing important work in Kibera. In their newsletter, Plan employees say that some 17-year-olds do not know what menstruation means and continues that in some areas of Kibera, up to eight out of ten girls get pregnant before finishing school. Plan and their partners hold trainings for girls in the region about sexual and reproductive health and rights, so that they get the right information and more opportunities to influence their future. International Menstruation Day is celebrated annually on May 28.

800 million people have their periods every day. Still, menstrual taboos and lack of information about menstruation limit the lives of millions of girls and young women around the world. This needs to be changed. Improving the status of women is one of the most important ways to raise the living conditions of developing countries socially and in an ecologically sustainable way.

Mr. Trust

Our little Kenyan girl is waiting for us. We visit the office of the adoption organization to fill out documents and hear about the adoption process even before we get to the orphanage to meet Melissa. We need to visit the orphanage to get to know Melissa for a couple of hours a day for two weeks before we can bring her home with us. I'm excited, now everything really starts.

Even before leaving for the orphanage, I have one important task. I have to figure out the logistics for my work. I wouldn't be able to travel by matatu. Matatu are vans that transport people like buses. Matatu are typically Japanese vans with three rows of seats for passengers. The competition for passengers is sometimes loud and the pace is fast. A financier may be seen hanging outside from a moving car outside, attracting new customers. The number of seats seems to be indicative; the cars always seem to be full. Music is often played loudly to attract the attention of potential customers. Unfortunately, there have been a lot of accidents and one of the first instructions from the adoption organization is to avoid traveling by matatu. Since then, new bigger minibuses have been introduced in Nairobi to replace matatus. New vans are no longer allowed to be used in the city's traffic, so this form of transport will eventually disappear as the fleet runs out.

My employer, as a seasoned visitor to Africa, has advised that my best bet would be a taxi driver that I could completely trust. I thought about how such trust could be created quickly. So that both would benefit from the trust. Is there anything I could offer a reliable person, could I maybe teach him some knowledge or skill? We use more taxis at the beginning, and I talk a lot with the drivers. It's safe when Petri is with me. In my work, I would have to travel alone for longer journeys with a driver, maybe even in the dark, so we would have to find a reliable person. I also want him to get along well with Topias, meaning children in general. One day I notice a dark blue minivan in the parking lot of our neighbourhood shopping center and we get into it. The driver is calm and friendly. He is not a strong bodyguard-style type, but his strength is a thoughtful, negotiating, cooperative, solution-oriented attitude in all situations. Mr. Trust, I think. He also knows how to be natural with Topias. He wipes sweat from his forehead in the heat of the day. I watch as he tries diligently to get Topias' seat into the car. Petri helps him and Mr. Trust lifts the trusting Topias into the car with a gentle smile. He clearly has a genuine desire to help people. He is happy to answer all our questions and tries to find the answer even to those he doesn't know. He was calm and confident. He says: – My name is ..
- Nice to meet you. I'm Päivi. I reply.
In this book I will call him Mr. T.

Even on this first short trip, I ask for his phone number and say that we would need a taxi often. He says he drives a friend's car and is often at work, almost always. He would gladly transport us when we needed. If sometimes it he can't make it, one of his friends will come. This is exactly what I need. Mr. T's car is a brand new seven-seater Toyota, which is a refreshing exception from many taxis that have seen their best days. Every car in front of you is Toyota - the advertising slogan (which was read on the spare tire cover of a car standing in front of us) is very true in Nairobi's traffic. Taxis don't look the same, the cars typically don't have any taxi markings. Drivers hang out in shopping center parking lots waiting for rides. Very quickly, we learned to find the corner in the parking areas where the ride providers are waiting. On the other hand, Europeans sweating with shopping bags and small children won't have to look for a ride for long before transportation services will be offered. Before we left, we had a very clear vision of what we would demand from taxi rides from a safety point of view. In the end, sometimes we have to be flexible about these requirements. Even a malfunctioning seat belt does not prevent you from getting on board during rush hour, if in some acute situations you have to move from one place to another. Mr. T's taxi brings relief and a solution to this as well. In that car, we feel that we no longer need to compromise on safety and, thanks to the air conditioning, not on comfort either. Mr. T. also understands our need for safety when moving with children and never causes extra heartbeats with his driving style.

In the evening, I thought about how to open a conversation with Mr. T about a wider cooperation. Maybe we should talk about how we can support each other on this journey. The next morning, Mr. T. would pick me up to go to work. I need to think up something. The sun rises and I rush to find sunscreen. Mr. T. drives into the yard and I climb into the back seat. Now would be the moment, just have to say something. I bawled out:

- Could you support us during this scary journey?

Mr. T gets confused and answers: - Of course. He asks that what exactly I mean. I tell him that I need someone I can always count on, especially if I'm in trouble. Petri should be able to safely send me far from Nairobi.

- For my part, I want to reciprocally support you. I'm not rich, but could I teach you something?

I am asking if, for example, computer, internet and social media skills would be useful for Mr. T in terms of his future. Mr. T. is happy and says that it is a good idea. However, he doesn't have any days off, only on Sundays in connection with going to church, he would be able to arrange a little time to be taught. So that's what we agreed. Every Sunday with us. If necessary, Mr. T. could take his children with him to come to play and eat with us. Our close friendship starts from there. The foundation of trust has been built. Trust becomes vital on our journey. We order Mr. T to drive us whenever needed. We also recommend him to other adoptive families, and I agreed with Mr. T in advance about my work trips to ensure that he is available.

I ask my colleague about ambulances in case something surprising happens: - How do you order an ambulance in your home village? Is there a general emergency number?

I get a burst of laughter in response: - The ambulance service is provided by a bicycle belonging to one of the villagers, but if it has a flat tire, it cannot travel. In that case a donkey is used for transport to the hospital, but of course donkey doesn't listen, so getting to the hospital with it is more difficult.

I choose to turn to Mr. T in my time of need. He is our life insurance and our friend. I hope nothing happens. And if it does, at least now we have someone we can trust on for support and advice.

African Fairy

"I always whisper good night to you," said Piglet to Pooh.
"But we live on different sides of the forest," said Pooh.
"That's why. Then it feels like you're close." [9]

I can imagine in my mind Topias and Melissa having a similar conversation. We are already so close to his little sister, yet still miles away.

The gate of the orphanage opens. We drive in. We're all excited. Topias holds tightly to the Piglet plush toy that he could give to his little sister today. The orphanage is a two-story stone building. A dog sleeps in its yard and is outside at night guarding the area. The dog would surely have many stories to tell. A dog is the only real security for children at night. When it gets dark, the thick metal gates of the high fences surrounding the yard of the children's home are locked. Access to the building is blocked by metal bars on the windows, and the metal exterior doors are bolted from the inside. Possibly, only one adult will be left on duty for the night with fifty minor residents. The dog guards the yard against possible uninvited night visitors.

We don't really know what to expect from an orphanage. The children's home is located north of Nairobi, and it is run by a foreign couple, who run the operation largely thanks to donations from the Christian congregation from their home country. The adoptive parents of the children who are up for adoption pay the costs incurred for the child, but the orphanage does not make a profit from the adoption activities.

When we arrive at the children's home, the guard peeks through the small hatch in the metal gate, greets the contact person of the adoption organization who is coming with us, and opens the heavy gate. The children's home area has a large two-story main building, the ground floor of which has a kitchen, dining area, and living room. Right next to the gate is a small school building where we see small children in their lessons. The children living in the orphanage are lucky to have the opportunity to go to school, which is by no means a given for all disadvantaged Kenyan children. In the orphanage's own school, the lowest grades are taught, older children wear school uniforms and travel by bus to school outside the orphanage. The aim of the education is to secure children's readiness for an independent life outside the walls when coming of age. The orphanage also has its own well in the yard. Ensuring the water supply is certainly must in this extreme dry area. Even in the orphanage's well, the groundwater has already dropped threateningly. If only everyone in this world would remember to help those who are struggling with water scarcity.

As soon as we get out of the car, we are guided in from the front yard. The woman who received us leads us past the lounges and opens the door to the children's bedroom. In the bedroom we see a bed with a baby sleeping in the bassinet. Next to it is an empty crib. The nurse says it's Melissa's bed. The room also has three bunk beds and a lot of pots. Melissa sleeps with a few small children on the bottom floor of the main building next to the dining areas. Older children sleep upstairs. Upstairs is the children's personal area, where we visitors are not allowed. I see a boy from the window who is in a wheelchair in the shade in the side yard. He seems happy. The nurse says that in addition to adoptions, the orphanage is also able to treat this boy's illness with its fundraising from donors. To our surprise, not all children are orphans. The girl closest to Melissa is in an orphanage because her single mother cannot support the girl with her small income. The mother visits her daughter regularly, hoping that one day she will be able to provide a safe home for her child herself.

She is grateful that she has been able to find food, a roof over her head and the opportunity for education in an orphanage for her kid.

The nurse tells Melissa that she is in the yard, and heads to the door leading to the backyard. Now it's happening. My heart starts beating harder. How would the meeting go? I can't even imagine what it's like to meet your child under two years old for the first time abroad. Melissa understands English. I believe that everything will go well for sure. We follow the nurse towards the front door. Topias steps happily, but alertly, into the yard. Two sweet little Kenyan girls are swinging in the middle of the yard.

- That one on the left is Melissa. The nurse says.

Melissa is small, delicate and sweet like a beautiful fairy in fairy tales. Her hair is braided with black cotton thread and colourful beads, and the braids are pulled up into two ponytails on either side of her head. This is how the girl's own thick, curly hair has been brought under control. The girls look at us suspiciously but curiously. A road of twenty tiles leads to Melissa. Topias holds the Piglet soft toy in front of him and starts towards Melissa. I can only guess what goes through Topias' head when he sees his long-awaited little sister for the first time. Careful not to scare the little ones, Topias approaches Melissa. Melissa and the other girl have gotten used to strange families in the area of the orphanage and have learned to treat everyone with suspicion. Those strange adults have taken many children with them. As we approach Melissa, she narrows her brows. Petri and I stop a few meters away from the swings. From all strangers, girls only trust children. Topias continues forward alone and extends soft toy in his hands directly towards Melissa. Melissa notices the soft toy and smiles at her brother. Topias smiles back. The connection has been made! Topias puts Piglet in Melissa's arms. The girl's eyes are happy. I swallow so that my cry of happiness doesn't startle her. Topias carefully grabs one of the swing strings and rocks Melissa quietly. We are waiting. The minutes seem like an eternity. Suddenly, Melissa holds out both of her hands to Topias. With the strength of an almost five-year-old, Topias lifts Melissa from the swing.

Melissa's smile is still beyond our reach. However, the most important thing is that she trust Topias already. Our children's smiles are the sweetest in the world! The smiles of these children reach every corner of my heart, and the happiness of motherhood overwhelms me. Our beloved children!

We go visit the orphanage again on next day. In the yard of the orphanage, a boy about eleven years old grabs my hand and asks if we could take him with us. He has seen adopted children, children who have come to visit or heard that children who have left the orphanage are doing well in life. It's crushing to realize that it's not that easy for someone that age to have a family. He will probably grow up in an orphanage. We cannot help him in this matter. The law dictates how things go, so I try to make him happy by talking nice things and praising his skills. I try to convince him to believe in his own abilities, to tell him how nice he is and that he still has a good life ahead of him. Adoption is not charity, but a deep long-term wish and desire to have a child in one's own family. An adopted child should never have to owe his parents a debt of gratitude. Still, we face the need for help in Kenya every day. Along with the adoption process, we try to help locals as much as we can.

Melissa is playing in the sandbox with a little boy. Topias is immediately included in the play, and I sit quietly, soundlessly, on the edge of the sandbox. Topias is talking to me, and Melissa and the little boy are observing the situation. Slowly I go to take a sand toy and show how you can make a cake with it. That's when Melissa smiles at me for the first time. Oh, what a captivating smile. Now I got to experience it too! The smile is very careful and sweet. Suddenly, Melissa grabs me by the braids and curiously explores my different hair with her little fingers. My long, brown hair is spiky and slick.

They are different from what he and other Kenyans are used to. The building of trust has begun.

Our daily playtimes at the children's home would last about two weeks. I could be there whole day from morning to night, but the orphanage has its own planned schedule. In addition to playing, we get to feed the happy Melissa in the baby chair. Topias and Melissa have fun when Topias tries to spoon banana-bean baby food into Melissa's mouth. Days pass and little by little Melissa starts to trust us. She understands that we only want good for her.

For two weeks, the white minibus of the Little Angels adoption organization will pick us up from our apartment in the mornings. We travel about an hour to the other side of the city, and we usually get there before the children's lunch time. The orphanage has a menu for a week with different meals for each day. There is no meat available. On Sundays, after the church service, there is spaghetti and a special delicacy, milk. The same menu is repeated every week. The children's home's two cooks prepare the meals. The children take care of setting and cleaning the tables. Older children distribute food to each table. Before the meal, the children read the food prayer in unison. The meal has a warm, communal and safe atmosphere.

We managed to watch the children's activities in the yard while getting to know our daughter at the same time. The children run along the flat grassy yard playing hopscotch, hide and seek and kicking the ball. They act just like children around the world in yards and parks. Watching their joy, we forget that they are orphans, they are all just children.

When Topias and Melissa are not sitting on the swings, Petri and I sit on the edge of the sandbox playing with Melissa and her friends. There are hardly any toys. We sit smiling, talk soothingly to Melissa and marvel at our luck. Older children study us with interest. After a couple of visits to orphanage, the bravest ones come to talk to us adults, asking where we are from. They want to know if Melissa is going with us, how old we are and what we are doing in our home country. Those and many other questions cross the children's lively conversation with us. We patiently answer the endless flow of questions.

Today is the day Melissa would go home with us to Nairobi. According to adoption counselling, it will be a difficult moment that will tear Melissa from everything she's used to. We are taking her away from the children she has grown up with and who are the most important and the greatest security for her in her little world. Understanding this was helped by the imagery exercise we did in adoption counselling, where we would be taken from home to a palace to all the gold and glitter. Still, we would miss home and our family, just as Melissa will miss the children who have become her family.

Before leaving, the orphanage has an important ritual: weighing the departing child. We would visit the orphanage every month until the end of the adoption process, and each time Melissa would be put on the scale to be weighed. No other health-related monitoring is done, as weight development is the only decisive factor.

We get permission from the director of the orphanage to leave with Melissa. I look at Petri meaningfully and Petri instructs Topias that the quick departure we've been talking about will soon take place. Topias nods and they start hand in hand towards the car. I pick Melissa up in my arms and calmly start walking away from the other children, holding back my tears. Melissa begins to furrow her brows in concern. Now we have to act fast. We are directed towards the car. As Melissa realizes that the distance from the other children is growing, she starts to scream and squeal hysterically. I lift Melissa in my arms into the car because there is no way we can put her put in a car seat. We would only try that outside the children's home area after the gates have closed. I hold Melissa, gently press her against me, we both cry. I try to calm her down in the back of the minivan as it backs out of the orphanage gates. Topias is also worried but understands the situation we have trained him for. Topias does everything to make Melissa feel better. He tries to hand out toys and cookies. Petri comforts Topias and they both have tears in their eyes as well. The drive home feels like an eternity. Melissa eventually gets tired of crying and ranting. She has his middle finger and ring finger in her mouth and is sweaty all over.

Melissa is our little fairy princess. I try to give her juice and get her to drink a little. We arrive at the gates of our estate. There are adoptive families in the yard. Everyone is happy for us, as we have been happy for them, who have already had their own child. We also share in spirit the excitement of those who are still waiting to meet their own child. We quickly sneak into our apartment so that Melissa can have a chance calm down with us.

We immediately give Melissa bread and milk, which she likes. Melissa could now eat and drink as much as she wanted. We will do whatever it takes to make Melissa feel better. In the evening, the smile has already returned to her face. Melissa's first word in Finnish is "pä" sorter from 'leipä', which she means bread. We clap and cheer together when she said it and she happily repeats it over and over again.

As bedtime approaches, Topias shows Melissa soft toys in the bedroom. Topias goes to his own bed, and I carefully try to put Melissa in the crib next to him. We have borrowed a similar wooden, light brown crib, from orphanage in which Melissa had slept her first years. She immediately starts shaking and crying loudly. I take her in my arms and sit on the bed next to me. Melissa calms down to sob in my arms. Finally, she falls asleep. I wait 15 minutes and carefully try to move Melissa to bed. The crying starts immediately. I am thankful that we got this child and with time we will get her to recover from the shock.

Later we ask Mr T to take our whole family to visit the orphanage. On the way, we pass extensive coffee and tea plantations. On one such trip, we ask our driver to go between the coffee plantations. We look at endless plantations and collection areas where fresh white coffee beans are piled on metal sheets to dry in the sun. Inside the red coffee berry are two light coffee beans. At first glance, this seemed incredible. I have strong memory from ad that was playing in television when I was younger. In the ad, a happy coffee farmer collects beautiful brown coffee beans from his plantation located on a mountain wall and a straw backpack he carries on his back. In this way, we consumers are fed images that fuel buying. The small white berry doesn't go together with the roasted, dark coffee feel.

The drastic continuation of the immutability of family conditions required by adoption counselling in Kenya, is the stagnation of time, the waiting, where once again we do not know how long it will last. We live under a magnifying glass inside a wall. Before the trial begins, the social workers visit our home for three months. There is no information on trials' duration. We hear the time estimate varies from less than six months to more than a year. The family court sits only one morning once a week. It is sometimes difficult to get a processing time, and due to court schedules, the waiting time can add weeks more in an instant. The court will proceed only under the presiding of a certain named judge. If the judge has something else to do, there is no other option but to apply for a new hearing time for the next free day that could be weeks later. For me, the waiting time is not so heavy when I work, but for Petri, every day is the same: cooking, laundry, outdoor activities at the pool, naps, shopping trips, more cooking and washing dishes. Topias will also soon start thinking about returning home, it's hard to explain to him that we don't know for sure when we'll be back. We make a huge calendar on the wall of his room, from which we remove one box every morning. We set going home date in

June. We don't know the day for sure, but we had to come up with something to calm him down. We need to start coming up with other things to do for the kids.

At home, we hold daily happy lotion- discos, due Melissa's dry skin has to be lined with thick lotion every day from head to toe. When dancing, she can wait for the lotion to be absorbed. Topias is excited to dance with his sister and everyone has a good time. Now you can clearly see how much and how long Topias has been waiting for his sibling. Disco hits from the 90s are playing in kids' smurf versions that gets children in happy mood and dancing and that make us dance too. When everything outside the home is regulated, in our own home we try to rejoice in our free time.

We also organize fun events for children with other adoptive families. We celebrate Melissa's two-year birthday together with another adopted child. All children and many of us parents dress up in costumes.

Locusts. One day we wonder when the walls of our own local shopping mall and the whole ground outside it are full of neon light green locusts. We see with Mr. T how a local family collects these large locusts in sacks from the nearby bush. Mr. T. says that grasshoppers cause a lot of destruction, but also provide a good source of protein. While I was writing this book, a start-up has figured out that crickets could be used as feed for animals. In 2020, the Horn of Africa and Kenya saw the worst locust invasions in seventy years. Unusual weather phenomena and climate change created favourable conditions for crickets. Heavy rains made them swarm and hurricanes spread them over a wide area.

We sometimes invite Mr. T to eat with us and offer him a meal, because otherwise he would be sitting in the car in the parking lot waiting for us to return. On one of these occasions, I look at the meat dishes and bubbling cola drinks served in front of us. I thought about the family that collected grasshoppers. What does Mr. T. really think about our life, which must seem so easy and abundant to him? However, at the same time, we ourselves feel that there are big problems and challenges in our lives. Mr. T. is an empathetic person, and we can talk with him completely openly about both our situation and the challenges of the locals separately without comparing them to each other.

Kenya's nature is amazing, and we want to get to know it while living there. Topias and Petri go on a mountain trip to the nearby Ngong hills with warriors from the Masai tribe. The warrior acting as a guide says that there are African buffalo roaming the hills, which are said to be one of the most dangerous animals in Kenya. A man dressed as a Masai warrior with a rudimentary looking bow-gun doesn't seem like much protection against African buffalo. Petri suspects that he is protecting us from a much more dangerous animal. According to rumours, Westerners camping in Ngong mountain have sometimes had all their belongings stolen, including their underwear.

The highest peak of the Ngong Hills rises to a height of about 2,460 meters above sea level. An easily accessible path leads to the top. In addition to the bushes growing on the slope, grass up to half the thigh grows on the slope. Topias is riding on Petri's back along the steep path towards the top of the mountain. At some point, both think that it would be good for Topias to walk a little while. The boy steps off the chest and sits down on the ground to rest. Almost immediately, he jumps screaming into the air. The adults around wonder what has happened. Routinely, our guide begins to remove and shake Topias' outer clothing: – Safari ants. Their bite feels worse than a wasp sting.

With Petri's help, Topias can be moved from the path of the ants and the clothes can be cleaned of the fierce biting ants. After a while, Topias is safely back on his father's back and the journey can continue. At the top, Petri and Topias arrive at a wide plateau, which ends abruptly in a steep and almost 1,000-meter drop, the East African rift valley. The view over the mankinds' birthplace is an indescribable experience.

After seeing the rift valley, Petri, who is interested in science, takes our family to the Natural History Museum in Nairobi to see an exhibition about the early humans and the history of human evolution. While visiting a natural history museum, we hear the guide tell a group of schoolchildren on a class trip that black thin snakes in front of a terrarium, they are so-called thirty-minute snakes. The snakes in question are black mambas. The name comes from their completely black mouth. Apparently, a bite from this snake kills in thirty minutes without antidote. We are left to wonder what it would be like to live in a simple dwelling where such animals would seek shelter.

Tourisms and trips

With another adoptive family, we decide to rent a house for the weekend near Naivasha - a lake located about two hours' drive from Nairobi. The road between Nairobi and Lake Naivasha is remarkably good and wide. On the side of the road stands a sign familiar from European highways: "Financed in part with the support of the European Union". Around Lake Naivasha, there are numerous flower farms owned by Europeans, which produce a large part of Europe's imported flowers. The flowers produced around the lake are picked, loaded and transported by road to Nairobi Airport. From there, they fly to flower wholesalers in the Netherlands and from there to Finland, for example, as Fair Trade-roses.

The kids start calling the place the Chicken Home because there are chickens running free in the property's high-walled yard. We will be sleeping under a malaria nets after long time, because there has been no need for it in Nairobi. The house is spacious, the yard is large and there is a private swimming pool next to the house. Melissa pushes Topias and another family's adopted son on the yard road on a children's tandem bike. The bike's tires sink into the soft sand, but Melissa continues to push vigorously. The girl I thought was a fairy proves to be as strong as Pippi Longstocking.

We go to take a closer look at the nearby village and decide to eat at a local restaurant. We enter to examine the menus hanging on the walls. The proximity to Lake Naivasha is reflected in the menu, which offers significantly more fish than in restaurants in Nairobi. Fish Perch-like fish, tilapia, is available on the market in many different forms. The fish in question is not familiar to us, but after returning to Finland, we notice that it is regularly offered in ethnic shops. The group dining at a nearby table turns their attention to us and the loud African children with us: - Why do you have that girl with you? Where is that girl's mother? Take that child to his parents!

We understand that international adoption is not something that is familiar or desirable to all Kenyans. We leave the restaurant with the least amount of noise and decide to eat at our holiday apartment that evening as well.

The rented property is large. In addition to the actual apartment and the swimming pool area, there are a few outbuildings on the plot, as usual, all inside high walls. We wander around the area to pass the time and find a big pit behind one of the buildings where the waste left by guests is burned. Food waste, plastic and even glass and metal waste are dumped in the same bin. The smell rising from the pit is already familiar from Nairobi. In the absence of waste management, burning all household waste is a very common practice.

Naivasha National Park is one of the few places where it is possible to walk in nature, because there are no feline predators. Despite that, we don't dare to go out into the countryside with the children, instead the men only go to explore the park on foot. Being outside in nature is really a different experience. The nature park has vast steppes full of zebras and wonderful dried riverbeds carved into the limestone by the water, where you can walk for long distances. Goats and young shepherd boys herding them climb the steep cliffs. Petri, dressed in hiking boots, wonders how the boys can balance with worn-out plastic Crocs imitations on the walls.

After a relaxing weekend, we leave back to our home in Nairobi with the transportation provided by the company that we rented the house from. In addition to the driver, there is another man in the front seat to ensure our safety. Petri and I sit behind the driver and the security guard in the next row of seats, Melissa sits between us. There is no real place for Topias, but the driver has built an extra seat on the front seat next to him, where he directs Topias. After driving some distance, men with big guns appear from the side of the road in front of our car. I quickly put my jacket over Melissa and we wait. Petri stealthily digs out a note from between his passport, which he has put there for these possible situations. We had read that Kenya was the 138th most corrupt country in the world. Money is a small price for us to be able to continue the journey safely. I'm scared for Topias. He has never seen guns. We've purposely never gotten him toy guns, and that unexpectedly turns out to be our win. Topias remembers what we have taught him to say when we have had Kenyan social workers visit our home. He quickly stretches out his hand towards the policeman who is leaning on the window frame of the car with his submachine gun and says:
– I am Topias, I am five.

The men look confused at Topias, who is smiling fearlessly with her big blue eyes. The men back off and motion that we can continue our journey. The journey continues safely towards home.

After a few days, Mr. T and I are driving home from a work meeting together late in the evening. We didn't manage to leave in time and we get stuck in traffic. It's seven o'clock and it's already getting dark. In front of our house, the line of cars slows down, and as if out of nowhere, a crowd of people appears around the cars. They have sticks, picks and burning torches. Everyone is shouting loudly; I can't make out what they want. The crowd pushes and kicks cars stopped in line, including our car.

– What should we do now? I ask Mr. T worriedly.

- It's okay, we're not their target, we'll move on soon. Mr. T. calms me down and continues: - I don't know what they are protesting against here, but this is a fairly ordinary demonstration.

We wait in silence as the car sways from side to side. I hope the glass of the window can withstand the blows and pushes of the crowd of people passing by. I look past the flickering brightly burning torches and I return in my mind to the scout cabin years ago, the gang that appeared outside and set the tree next to the cabin on fire. I look outside at the surroundings and how, in which direction I would need to go, in case someone sets our car on fire. The crowd disperses as suddenly as it appeared, and the line of cars now finally starts moving. Fortunately, we are next to home! We turn onto the courtyard road and the gates of our dormitory open. Home again. I take a few deep breaths before saying goodbye to Mr. T, getting out of the car in the parking lot of our yard, and walking to the front door.

We are the whole family in the countryside in Mr. T's car, returning from the giraffe park, where we had been able to feed the giraffes from the stage, we saw wild pigs and big land turtles. We had a surprising opportunity to walk as a family through the fenced nature trail located in the area of the giraffe park. How liberating it had been to move in nature without anyone outside! I stare out the car window and notice our pace starting to slow down. I notice Petri sitting next to me looking around, trying to figure out why Mr. T steers the car to the side of the road. The car stops and the engine shuts off. Mr. T stares at the panel in agony and turns the car key in the ignition repeatedly. The starter motor makes a familiar noise, but the car won't start again.

- What's wrong? I'll ask our driver.

He remains silent and continues to turn the key. After a few tries, he stops and slouches in his seat.

– Is the car broken? Petri asks.

Mr. T looks at us worriedly through the rear mirror: - No. Apparently, we're out of gas. I'll go get some more.

We watch as he gets out of the car, takes a plastic gasoline can from the trunk, locks the doors and hands the car keys to Petri through the window crack.

- This may take time, don't worry, I will come to pick you up. Just remember not to open the doors under any circumstances.

Mr. T takes a couple of running steps across the road and signals the approaching matatu to stop. In no time, he has climbed into the car with the canisters, and we are left on the side of the road by ourselves. Petri and I look at each other confused. We are stuck in a car along the Kenyan roads with our children for an undetermined amount of time. Everything happens so fast that I only realize after Mr. T jumps into the matatu that we only have half a liter of water in the bottle. At first everything goes well. We undress the children because it's getting hot in the car. Melissa is only in a diaper now. In the end, it's so hot that we would need to open the doors but we don't dare. People passing by slow down at us and peek inside the car, wondering at the sounds of children coming from the car. We distribute water to children. Melissa is getting restless and Topias is also visibly in pain. I start playing singing games for the children, another half hour will pass.

109

It's 27 degrees outside. As the children's exhaustion and anxiety increase, the number of people stopping outside the car increases. We smile at passers-by wet with sweat and motion them to continue their journey. Finally, I see a cloud of sand dust, with a matatu curving from the middle to the side of the road. Mr. T. comes with a gas canister. Fortunately, you can always count on him. Mr. T is quiet during the journey home. I assure him that everything is fine and that similar things happen to everyone. I will notice that there is plenty of gas in the gas tank on the next trips. In the future, our trip would no longer be interrupted by running out of fuel.

Amid everything that is happening, we always have a certain relaxed attitude, especially in stressful situations, and we plan instead of panicking about unexpected events. I thought about where this character trait comes from, and I immediately see my parents in my eyes. In the middle of the renovation of our childhood house, the little things might not be as they should, as long as the most important things (like water for the children in a hot car in Kenya) are in order and the direction is clear. We will get through everything! Maybe not right away, and maybe not the way we had thought, but it will turn out for the best, as it says in the card, I bought later for Topias. In my opinion, not giving up is that if there is no route, you find it or do it yourself!

My parents, who don't know the English, already decided after hearing about our departure to Kenya that they will come to meet us in Nairobi. They have no idea how they would survive changing planes without language skills, but the attitude is right. My parents have always been brave. Already when they were younger, they moved together from a small town from Northern Finland to Helsinki and soon became furniture entrepreneurs.

I dictate to my parents to take a note in English that says where they are going. They could show this text at airports in situations where they don't know to go, to get the service they need on the plane, to find their way to their bags, and to get out of the airport in Nairobi. Mr. T and Petri would meet them.

We all fit in Mr. T's minivan and do a lot of hiking together while my parents are visiting. Especially the safari is impressive. Just outside the city, a vast savannah area opens, where we see crocodiles, giraffes, felines and other savannah animals. We eagerly try to get Topias to look at the wonderful big animals, but Topias has already noticed an interesting wild animal on the floor of the car. He happily points to an ant squirming at his feet and closely follows a small insect across the sky on the floor of the safari bus while the rest of us peer at a rhinoceros feeding some distance away. Topias's enthusiasm for the ant lasts longer than us adults for the rhinoceros. After a while we were all crouching on the floor of the car admiring the ants in the company of a proud Topias.

When we leave the nature park, we still get to follow the traditional song of the Masai warriors bouncing in the air in rhythm at the gates. According to Maasai tradition, two front lower teeth are knocked out from children so that the person can be fed in case of tetanus. Missing teeth are as characteristic features as their red clothes and their shields and spears depicted on the Kenyan flag.

Time with my parents is a great change from everyday life. I'm happy that they too get to see what our life is like here south of the equator. Life goes on as a reasonably normal everyday life and the security concerns that filled our heads before our departure have largely disappeared, at least temporarily.

My parents and I are returning from the city in Mr. T's ride, when suddenly a car pulls into our own lane slowly and uncertainly. Mr. T stops the car and blows the horn. The oncoming car continues its journey until it finally crashes into our minibus. Once again, I congratulate myself for taking the trouble to find a safe ride when we arrived. We look through the windshield at the driver who hit us and see a woman behind the wheel who is in completely different worlds. Mr. T gets out of the car to check the damage, tells us the driver is high from drugs and glances in our direction.

Fortunately, the speed of the collision was slow, the adults were wearing seat belts and the children were in car seats, so we avoided personal injury in a head-on collision. Our driver quickly walks over to the driver of the other car, opens the door and grabs the car keys before calling the police. The police arrive surprisingly quickly, and Mr. T settles the matter with the police. They look at the front of our car, record the damage and, in front of the eyes of the other car, take the confused driver into the back seat of the police car. We finally get to continue our journey. Mr. T gets behind the wheel, starts the car and says: - Everything is fine. There was no major damage to the car and I can drive you home.

- Was that other driver okay? I ask Mr. T as the car starts to move.

- Yes, he was. He may not be doing very well at the police department. He continues quietly, as if talking to himself.

I'm left thinking about Mr. T's comment about the police station. I have had no dealings with the police while we have been in Kenya. Petri had previously gone to the nearby police station to file a criminal report for the insurance company about the things that were missing from our suitcases. Our bags that were lost in London were delivered to Nairobi three weeks after our arrival and we noticed that clothes and electronics were missing from them. Petri was directed to talk to a criminal investigator, who excitedly told about a Finnish acquaintance of his who visits Kenya regularly. - You Finns insure everything just in case. He laughed about his experiences of conversations with an acquaintance and put his stamp on the criminal report. The visit was over in a few minutes. In Petri's opinion, the experience was mainly hilarious, not scary or unpleasant in any way. So maybe I would also dare to do business at the police station if the situation demanded it, but at least I would take Mr. T with me in that case.

112

On the last evening before my parents leave for Finland, we go to eat at a cozy restaurant near the Nairobi Nature Park. We ask Mr. T to eat with us as we want to serve him dinner. Mr. T. is surprised, but happily comes with us to the restaurant. I thought about how Mr. T. feels about it now, but I still don't dare to ask. He smiles now as usual, but somehow behind the smile there is often a lot of worry and sadness. A genuine smile is rarely found. Especially today in his eyes you can see his wish that one day he could offer the same meal to everyone. That's what I hope too.

Life on the film tape

In our home in Kenya, we also have guests, other adoptive families and my local colleagues with their acquaintances. Someone has left a bottle of nail polish remover in our kitchen waste bin without us noticing. As a curious and eager girl, Melissa picks the bottle from the garbage. Noticing Melissa looking at the bottle, I immediately raise the trash can higher. At that point I don't realize at that it's a nail polish remover, and especially not that Melissa had unscrewed the bottle's cap a little earlier and poured the substance at the bottom of the bottle into her mouth. After moving the trash can to a safe place, I lift Melissa into my arms. I notice her breath smells of acetone. I immediately call my mother in Finland to ask the hospital what we need to do next. How toxic is nail polish remover? The hospital says that if swallowed, it is not as toxic as if inhaled, but Melissa needs to get a chest X-ray quickly. I call Mr. T again and ask him to come urgently. We drive quickly to the hospital. Mr. T tells me I have to rescue him then if we get caught speeding. I promise to pay the fines if we get Melissa help in time. The pain of losing comes to the surface again. Melissa has to survive; this can't end here. Mr. T drives like a lunatic. Our credit driver, who normally drives calmly, knows how to take advantage of every passing place if necessary. The journey to the hospital door is over in a few moments. We quickly get to the lung scan, which luckily, we get over it only with a scare. Mr. T waits with me in the waiting room until Melissa gets out of observation and then drives us home in his usual calm style.

Everyday life continues with work. I'm going to a working lunch with our partner at a restaurant owned by a Dutch chain. Everything is so familiar and safe European. Only later do I understand that the feeling of security was false. Everything works as we are used to in Finland, quickly and we get what we order. When we pay, the waiter chats nicely. He's obviously trying to make sure I don't notice the credit card machine left behind the countertop. I notice it and make sure the card is inserted into the device. I want to make sure my card doesn't get lost anywhere. The payment takes a little longer than normal, but after getting my card back and checking the invoice that everything is as per my order, I'm satisfied and don't think more of it.

The long rains meaning the rainy season on spring begins and the rain seems endless for a while. On one side of the plot of our residential building runs a deep and wide ditch, which turns into a flowing river. The force of the water wears away the embankments of the ditch and eventually takes away part of the grassy area of our yard. With that wall, the metal fence that protected the plot will remain partially hanging in the air over the ditch. The landslide is small, but the hole is big enough that a child could fall into the water. When the rain stops, we notice that part of the yard has disappeared when we go outside. Topias is very interested in the situation. He marvels at the torn lawn and digs a small hole a safe distance away from it. In addition to the shovel, he uses his hands to dig and investigates at the root that has appeared. Probably Topias wiped his nose or mouth with his dirty hands like children do when playing. In the evening, Topias starts vomiting violently. When the skin turns yellow, I call Mr. T again. Together, we decide over the phone that we should go to the hospital quickly now and that Mr. T will pick us up in his car.

The whole of Nairobi and all the surrounding areas are in chaos. The saying "pouring rain" fits here. I hadn't seen that happen before tonight in Nairobi. As the rain whips the minivan's glasses in the dark, the yellow of Topias's face takes on fiery hues.

- Please stay alive, we'll be at the hospital soon. I tell Topias.

He doesn't answer anything. Topias is breathing even though he is otherwise completely limp, pale and for some strange reason yellow. Could there have been something in the hole that Topias dug in the yard of our dormitory? – How much longer? I ask, shouting.

My voice is drowned out by the distress of the people outside the car. Mothers try to hold on to their children as large masses of water break the shore. Men lead goats and other animals to safety. The road is now just a muddy field. - It will take a while, will Topias manage? The sound comes from the front seat.

Before I could answer, Mr. T continued: - You know, some 8-year-old had already been washed away with the water. It should not be like this here, I guess this is due climate change. I look at my sweet little child. Hold on. My tears wet the T-shirt with a car print of his favourite movie. Tonight, the back seat of Mr. T's car is the scene of my child's fight for survival. My exhaustion and desperation bring the figure in black to the front seat next to Mr. T. I can see the female figure in my mind more clearly than ever. She has the same mischievous smile as before. She is manifestations of my fears.

Petri is at home with Melissa while I travel through rainy Nairobi in Mr. T's car towards the hospital. The journey seems to last forever. The rain is getting stronger, and it's pitch black. Traffic on the curvy road is at a standstill and the chaos outside the car continues. I'm afraid if Topias will make it all the way to the hospital. Mr. T concentrates on getting past the muddy little stream so that we could move forward in a hurry. A trip of less than an hour takes three hours in the end. I wondered how long the trip would have taken in this weather on a bicycle or on a donkey. In front of the hospital, we run into the lobby with Topias in our arms. Mr. T tells the staff the situation and Topias is quickly put on tubes. The inflammation level is skyrocketing, and the situation is serious. The bacterium has apparently come from the soil when the children were playing and digging in the yard of our house, as I feared. The doctor asks me to pay for the treatment right away, as it is customary here. I dig out my credit card. The receptionist swipes the card several times, but the result is the same every time: payment declined. Crying in my throat, I am begging that Topias wouldn't be taken off the tubes.

I call Petri, who checks the status of the card in the online bank. He notices that 4,000 euros worth of purchases have been made with the card without our knowledge and the credit limit appears to be zero. Four 1,000 euro purchases, expensive suits and electronics, items that can easily be resold have been quickly purchased with the card. I have used my credit card carefully only in trusted places. I immediately realized that my card had been copied at the restaurant, where the payment had taken longer than normal. Petri runs to knock on the door of another Finnish adoptive family with Melissa in his arms. The father of the family promises to leave in the dark of night to pay for Topias' treatment with our other card. We are grateful to the family.

We assure Mr T at the hospital reception that the second payment card will arrive very soon. We will succeed in our plea and my child's care will not be interrupted. Our friend finally arrives with another credit card and the hospital visit is paid for. I must stay at the hospital with Topias. I'm worried because Mr. T can't stay there. - We give you a room in a quiet wing. The nurse comforts. In a remote place, we would at least be unsafe. I anxiously look at Mr. T: – What if Topias is caught or something happens to me?

Mr. T solves the situation again and says: - I will send a man from our own tribe to the hospital for your safety. You can trust him completely.

I have learned a lot about tribes on this trip. There are 42 tribes in Kenya and their mutual relations vary. I learned at this point that if Mr. T says his tribe will help, I can count on that help. There's something great about community, keeping promises. Perhaps we have lost that in our developed society due to urbanization.

At night, Topias sleeps in a hospital bed. I get on the bed next to him. I take off my long sleeve shirt and long pants and tie us together at the wrists and ankles. That way, no one would be able to grab him without waking me up.

- Good night! I say with a loud voice.

A strong man's voice answers from behind the door: - Good night, madam.

I'm going to sleep. I wake up several times during the night and ask: - Are you still there? I always get the same safe answer: - I'm here, you can sleep, good night, madam.

I wake up happily to the first rays of the morning sun. We survived the night and I call Petri. He says that he and Melissa are already in Mr. T's car on the way to the hospital. We could soon switch places and Petri will stay in the hospital with Topias for the next few nights. I slide into the back seat of Mr. T's car next to Melissa. Finally, my nightmare is over.

Topias' inflammation value starts to decrease. We've already overcome many setbacks on our journey, I'm starting to believe that this too will be sorted out. The fear of losing my children has stayed with me since the first miscarriage, and it hasn't gotten any easier during our trip. The day after tomorrow, Topias would be released from the hospital. The next morning, Mr. T and I would go to the local police station to file a crime report in order to report the transactions of the copied card to the credit card company.

In the morning we drive to the police station yard. Low stone buildings frame the sandy parking area filled with the familiar red dust. Directly in front of us is the door to the reception. We enter through a rough doorway built of logs. Petri has been to the same police station before to make a report about the items missing from our suitcases. The criminal investigator's question, how can Petri know that the goods have not already been stolen in Helsinki, aroused some amusement in Petri. Of course, it could not be denied or even known. The criminal investigator had offered Petri tea and the conversation had progressed in a lighter tone towards the end.

In front of me is a table where the receptionist is writing Criminal events in a large A1-sized book with a fountain pen. Behind the clerk, there is an area separated from the room by bars, where people arrested on previous night sit on the floor awaiting further processing. Some are clearly confused from some intoxicants; some are even aggressive. It feels scary, even though there are bars in between. I begin to tell the events that will be recorded in the big book according to my speech. The official finally states that since it is such a large amount of money by local standards, we would have to go to the Financial Crimes Unit in Nairobi to investigate the matter. A Kenyan's monthly salary is around 30-60 euros. When we get there, they don't know how to help us either, by end of the day we end up visiting a total of thirteen different places.

At the last agency, as the evening is already approaching, it is stated that we need to handle this at our own local police station. Mr. T and I sigh deeply and return to the starting point. When we return, we tell the same receptionist what kind of day we had and what kind of instructions we had received. He doesn't know what to do next, so he directs us to the door to the right of the reception desk. I knock quietly and a husky male voice invites us inside

We enter a room where the main police chief sits behind his huge desk. In front of him on a small stool sits a thin, small man with his head bent. The police chief orders him to the bench by the wall when he sees us and beckons me to sit on the stool with his hand. Mr. T sits near me on the wall. I greet a new person casually and cheerfully, without any prejudice, just like in Finnish offices. Here, the same behaviour is obviously too relaxed because the police chief frowns. There are no signs of the smile.

- Evening. What has happened? The police chief asks and digs out a stack of A4-sized sheets and a fountain pen.

- We were here earlier in this morning, and we were sent to the centre of Nairobi to several places but were eventually directed back here. The whole event is recorded in the big book at the reception, so it can be found there. I say as matter-of-factly as possible and try to save the police chief time and effort, so he doesn't have to rewrite everything.

Surprisingly, he sharply answers back: - Are you going to advise me how I should do my own work?

I hastily answer that "I didn't..." and try to continue the sentence that I in no way meant anything bad, but the police chief interrupts my sentence in an angry voice saying: - You just did that!

I look at Mr. T startled, and his expression shows a mix of shock and fear. I realize that the situation now went too far by accident.

The police chief's gaze is thoughtful, but cruel at the same time. Unexpectedly, he writes "resisting public authority" on the paper under the heading of the crime. I'm terrified. I must have no indication anywhere that the adoption of my little darling girl will not be interrupted. During these months, Melissa has already fully become part of our family, Topias' long-awaited sibling. Will I be sued and what does that mean in Kenya? According to my colleagues, the value of the individual is something completely different here than what we are used to in Finland. The prisoners I saw in the holding cell come back to my mind too clearly. The detention cell in the lobby is terrible. If I somehow manage to get out of this room, no law would protect me at night in with that crazy group. The police chief taps the paper on the table with a pen and thinks. Tears are pouring down my cheeks and my head feels like the weight of a bowling ball. The silence is broken only by Mr. T's silent prayer in Swahili next to me. I realize that not even Mr. T can save me now. I'm starting to see visions of fear. I didn't know that watching your life flash before your eyes like a film strip was real, but now I believe it. All the happy events from childhood, safe moments, loved ones, even the dead, flash like images before my eyes. The film is interrupted by the police chief's absolute order to get up. I try to get up, but my legs won't carry me.

I lean back in my chair and look at the floor. What happens now? The police chief says something to Mr. T in Swahili. Mr. T grabs me by the arm and whispers that we're going right away. He pulls me out, I don't dare say anything. We head towards Mr. T's car.

- To the car now, quickly. Mr. T says and I get in the car. I ask in my distress: - Where are you taking me now, where am I going?

Mr. T drives a few hundred meters and looks in the rear mirror. He sighs deeply, stops the car and says: - We're going home now. You got another chance to come here tomorrow, provided you have a completely changed way of speaking and showing respect to the Chief of Police. No "Hello" is appropriate speech here, instead you must say "Dear Police Chief of X County, May I most humbly ask for permission to address you?" Do you understand, now we need to practice?

I thank him from the bottom of my heart for his help. We had to leave quickly in case the Chief of Police has change his mind, or that no one follow us. Mr. T saves me again from this situation too.

Early the next morning we go to the police station again. I enter the police chief's room with my head bowed and ask permission to speak. I get permission. I do exactly as Mr. T has instructed me and according to what the Chief of Police says at any given time. The

120

police chief records my story and then directs us to move to another building, where we would receive a certificate of filing a criminal report. We enter a smaller building where two police officers sit behind a desk. Mr. T tells them what the Chief of Police had instructed, and we are asked to sit down. They ask for proof of how much money has been taken. Petri has gone to a copy shop located in a nearby shopping center to print a statement from the online bank. I hand the statement across the table, satisfied that things are finally moving forward. I would probably soon get out of this distressing situation. The account statement shows the events about which I am now filing a criminal complaint. The police examine the bank statement carefully and then suggests that we go together to visit the online bank's branch in Nairobi to investigate the matter in more detail. I tell him that the online bank is, as its name suggests, an online service and that the Finnish bank offering the service does not have a branch in Nairobi.

- Then who gave you this account statement? The policeman asks furiously.

- I printed it myself. I'll explain to him.

- You cannot print bank documents yourself. The police say and repeat:

- Who gave you this document and in which office? What is the branch address? I explain it to Mr. T and he understands what I mean. He suggests that we draw how the information travels along the network. I will draw and explain what the internet is and how the online bank there works. The police are amazed, but luckily, they believe me in the end. Unexpectedly, the police announce that they should visit the restaurant that served as the scene of the crime. Unsuspecting, I offer them a ride in Mr. T's car. Mr. T moves strangely startled and I don't understand what is happening again. Mr. T asks for a stamp on the crime report certificate and suggests that the policemen get their coats and we would back the car up to the door ready for the policemen to get in the car. Great idea, I think and follow

Mr. T to the car. I barely had time to get into the car when Mr. T drove from the yard at high speed onto the road. He won't stop even when I yell that he forgot the cops. We're driving far again, and Mr. T is checking the rear mirror. I look behind, no one in sight. No one has followed us. Eventually he slows down and tells me that you should never go around crime scenes here with the police. They start visiting other restaurants and eating and drinking in them. At the end of the night, we would take the police home and pay the whole bill. At worst, they might have some made-up reason to arrest us. I gasp in disbelief, but I can tell by the look on Mr. T's face that this is true. I sigh and think that what would I do without him.

Now that I have a stamp on the criminal report, Petri is starting to work things out with the credit card company to get the stolen funds back from us. When inquiring to which address the crime report is sent, they tell us it is sufficient that we have made a crime report online to the Finnish police. There is therefore no need for a local crime report. This clarification would have been good to have when we first asked the credit card company for operating instructions. At least I now have this stamped paper and I'm one experience richer. Fortunately, one more stage of this adventure has been solved.

In addition to the police station, other officials also become familiar to us. One agency gets to know me too closely when, with Melissa on my back, I enter the women's room and suddenly the waste pipe running along the wall breaks and the sludge quickly floods the floor. Luckily, Melissa is safe on my back.

Nothing is as exciting as stepping into a courthouse. The courthouse is sterile in appearance, a large white stone building. Its courtyard has an open garden area, surrounded by open staircases running on three or four floors. We have made sure that everyone has appropriate and clean clothes and that the kids have enough snacks. I watch in the corridor as we wait for people to rush after the lawyers to different halls. When would it be our turn? Would we still have time to give the juices to the children? Topias is already impatiently waiting to sit on the bench in the courtroom with the headphones strap inside his shirt. Then his small gaming device would be quietly connected to the headphones, and he could play his favourite game. Melissa is waiting for the small cookies that we chopped up in a jar. The door to the room opens and our last names are called out. Now it's our turn.

At the first trial, attorneys are assigned to us, and the child and the process begins. In the second trial, it would be found that the process was successful, after which Petri and Topias would be free to leave for Finland already. In the final trial, the adoption would be confirmed and then Melissa would have all the necessary documents and then we would leave for Finland.

The second trial begins. We enter, sit on the bench and try to take care of the children's affairs in the row of benches quickly. We finish everything just as the judge, a stern-looking woman of around 50, comes behind her desk and knocks with a gavel to start the session. With a lump in our throat, we wonder how this will go. The judge examines the papers with assistants and asks questions of the lawyers, one representing us and one representing Melissa. This is the Kenyan practice in adoption cases. It's so quiet and formal that I don't even dare to change my position. I quickly glance sideways at the children and luckily both are silent.

We have ordered a suit for Petri at a local tailor and Topias too is dressed in his best. Suddenly, Melissa gets up and rushes away from the row of benches. I don't have time to catch her as she runs towards the judge's table. We are absolutely terrified. What happens now that we couldn't keep her to stay still? How is this treated here? The judge seems to be as confused as we are. Everyone is watching to see what Melissa will do next. Melissa points at me. The judge asks us to stand

123

up. My legs feel like spaghetti. The judge looks at Melissa and Melissa says in an audible voice in Finnish to the judge:

- Äiti! Melissa points at me at the same time. The judge asks me to tell in English what the child said. I will tell you that it is Finnish and means mother. The judge smiles at Melissa.

- Family Nuora, you are free to go home together as a family. The judge states and smiles at us.

The trial was short and happily ended thanks to the vivacious Melissa.

At the Boarder

We really miss Finland, our own home, relatives and friends. Summer is at its most beautiful in Finland and we decide that Petri and Topias will go to Finland first. It is again difficult to break up the family to live in different countries, but it is the best solution in this situation. When Petri and Topias fly to Finland, familiar landscapes are finally visible from the window. As the plane begins its descent, Petri points out the window at my parents' summer cabin by the lake to Topias. I have missed this country so much, Topias exclaims and makes everyone who understands Finnish in the nearby rows smile.

After the second trial, we have been in Kenya for six eventful months. After the boys leave for Finland, I will stay with Melissa in Kenya to wait for the last papers that we will receive in the third trial. My co-worker's sister promises to babysit Melissa while I work during the day.

We are moving in with another adoptive family so that it will be safer at night. The family helps take care of the children while I work. Kids like to play together. When we go to meetings with Mr. T, I take

Melissa and the nanny with me, I don't want to be in a different place than Melissa if something happens. In work meetings, the door is open and I can see them playing in the corridor.

A month and a half later, except for one piece of paper, everything is fine. I miss Finland very much. Many families have already successfully left for their home countries without this last piece of paper. I decide to try the same. It is hard to say goodbye to Mr. T and I would like to promise him that we will meet again. I have already given future adoptive families Mr. T's contact information and recommended him as an extremely reliable driver in every situation. Mr. T is doing well in his job regularly transporting European adoptive families, and he doesn't need to wait so much on the corner of the mall fishing for individual rides. What I completely miss is the bitterness and anger simmering beneath the surface that his success causes in other drivers. Petri has already said goodbye to Mr. T earlier. Petri gave a small tip for him, small amount to keep the family safe until we are all in Finland, but hopefully tells Mr. T how much we appreciate him.

We leave for the airport, firmly believing that we will get on the flight without the missing departure permit. Melissa sleeps on my back and I drag two large suitcases behind me. Melissa's papers are in a bag on my stomach so I can see them all the time. We arrive at the counter.

- You are missing one necessary document. The clerk states.

- Oh no. I think and ask what that document should say.

The official says that it ensures that I have permission to leave the country with the child: - You can't take your child out of the country against the will of his father.

- I have adopted her. I tell the clerk.

He replies rudely: - This is what everyone is trying to do, but we can see that your child looks just like you in terms of features. She is not adopted.

I try to show other documents, but they are not enough for a strict border officer. I suggest we could call the director of the orphanage. Fortunately, the clerk agrees and calls the children's home. The orphanage confirms that I have indeed adopted Melissa. The astonished clerk lets us board the flight.

When we land in Finland, I'm completely exhausted. First flight from Nairobi to London. At Heathrow, I transfer the next terminal for the Finnair flight with Melissa in my back and while dragging our luggage. Fortunately, Petri had carried most of our luggage with him, but managing even this amount of stuff is difficult when I have a little sleeping girl on my back at the same time. I've been trying to sleep on the flight with Melissa in my arms, but I haven't been able to sleep much. The flight from Nairobi via London to Helsinki has taken far too many hours. Exhausted, I get off the plane at Helsinki-Vantaa airport and drag our caravan along seemingly endless corridors. I notice the toilet and head there for a quick stop. A little relieved, I continue towards the border check with Melissa on my back. The border guard beckons us to the checkpoint and asks for papers. I fumble for my briefcase hanging over my stomach to realize it's gone. My tired brain can't remember where I could have forgotten the folder. I understand that I would not be able to enter the country with the child without the papers in the folder. My first reaction is to tell the border officer that I must have forgotten the documents on the plane. I feel the strain of the journey in my body. I feel like I couldn't handle the long walk back to the plane with a child on my back with all my luggage. I tell you that I am coming from a long adoption journey, and that my husband is waiting behind the wall. I ask if he could go investigate and get the documents after we get to him. The border guards say I can't get through the border until they can verify that I actually adopted Melissa:

- We see with our own eyes that she is your biological child.

I'm in the same situation again.

- You won't get through if we don't see the documents about the adoption. You have only one option, to retrieve the documents. They tell me.

Almost exhausted, I head back towards the plane. Despair is to gain power as my strength is fading. I perk up when I see the toilet like an oasis in the desert in front of me. Could the documents be there? At the same time, I get scared if I really forgot the documents there, and someone has taken them. What would I do then?

My steps quicken as I rush towards my previous stop. I quickly look around. There is no one in the room and I rush to the cubicle I used earlier. To my relief, I see a familiar document folder on the sink. I feel the exhaustion wash over me like a tidal wave. I pick up the folder tightly under my arm, take a breath, and head happily to the border again. This time the border guards welcome me and my children to Finland. Petri has already been waiting for a long time in the terminal and wondered where we are. Exhausted, I trudge through the entry gate with Melissa on my back, clutching my vital papers in my lap. I fall into Petri's arms. Finally, this journey is over and dear little Melissa is home in Finland.

We are heading straight to the summer house so that I can gather my strength for a few days before everyone at home wants to meet our long-awaited daughter. I realize that I hadn't eaten for almost a day while traveling from Nairobi to Helsinki. How heavenly ordinary and easy it feels when Petri turns on the way to the drive-in lane of a hamburger restaurant, before we continue our journey to our parents' summer house, where the grandparents together with the big brother are waiting for us. We are gathering strength for our first days together in Finland, to be able to introduce our new family member to everyone. Topias laughs at the happiness of seeing his sister after a break of more than a month. Everything is fine. The family is doing well and we are happy.

Murder

The last warm moments of the warm summer are at hand before the arrival of autumn.

I walk with Melissa and Topias to the playground near our home. They run ahead of the sandy footpath, and I happily walk behind. Topias sees familiar children on the playground's climbing frame. He yells in his bright five-year-old voice: - Hello everyone, this is my little sister I told you about! Her name is Melissa. Don't be surprised when she's all blue, it's because he comes from over there in Africa, Kenya. Topias didn't remember the skin colour right, which is so sweet it makes me smile. All the children take Melissa with them to play. With tears in my eyes, I happily sit on the bench to watch them play. Skin colours are indifferent to children, black, white, blue, purple.

Fortunately, my grandfather is still alive. The illness that started while we were living in Germany has not managed to take him down. I watch from the window of our house as he cycles into the yard. Instead of my parents or our home, grandfather always goes first to knock on the door of the playhouse: - Is the little lady of the house at home? He always exclaims kindly.

Melissa opens the door and happily brings a cup of dirt water from the yard to my grandfather and a nice sand cake decorated with leaves, stones and flowers. There is no better cafe than this.

Topias wants to go back to kindergarten with his friends right from the beginning of autumn. When applying for Topias, Melissa wants to join the children's games in the kindergarten yard and has a great time there. Melissa starts kindergarten at the end of the year when Petri returns to work. She makes a good friend in kindergarten, whose Kurdish mother came to Finland as a refugee from Iraq during

Saddam Hussein's regime. They are still friends to this day, ten years later.

One day, the kindergarten tells us that Melissa, who is otherwise always so sunny, has been sad and irritable all week. I notice the same at home. This continues for three weeks, and we can't figure out why, despite the joint efforts of the home and the day-care. No one has bullied Melissa. It seems that the reason for the bad feeling is found within her. In the evening we are going to sleep, Topias to his own bed and Melissa to hers. I sit between the beds to read a bedtime story. Suddenly, Melissa starts rocking herself back and forth in a sitting position. Topias and I look at the situation with confusion. I show Topias a finger in front of my mouth that we will be quiet. We'll keep an eye on what happens next. Melissa starts whining that she just kept swinging and swinging. She repeats it several dozen times. Topias is starting to look worried but doesn't say anything. Melissa stops and looks at Topias.

- Then Topias came and lifted me off the swing and then I got a dog! Melissa says, referring to our family's Welsh Springer Spaniel. Melissa smiles from ear to ear.

We all rejoice. Topias because he had made Melissa happy. I was happy to realize that Melissa was dealing with an important experience in her life. I myself learned more about adoptive motherhood with her. It's amazing to grow up with these kids.

It is important to notice the diversity of families and the various situations in everyone's everyday life. Everyday life won't always go as planned or as the majority assume things go with the children. Instead of bewilderment and disapproval, every family and child needs understanding. Instead of asking questions or, in the worst case, gossiping behind your back, what is needed is genuine empathetic listening and offering help. Understanding is needed from the parents in order to find together with the child the reason for his feelings. Often the child himself does not know where his fears come from, because they come so far from early childhood.

We have been happy when our children have always had safe circles of friends, and safe people around them who have given them good skills for life. However, our role has sometimes been tedious, because it is not always clear to us what the children's reactions or fears are. A lot of work has had to be done to understand our children and to make others understand what it is all about. You have had to build bridges between people in your new situations. We are forever grateful to everyone who has listened, understood and supported us and our children.

Murder. I can't believe what I'm hearing on the phone. I fall to sit on the bed. I don't even cry right away because the event sounds so unreal. The caller says that Mr. T has been stabbed to death on his own front gate. Dead. The finality of death, all the sadness, disbelief, anger, longing and other emotions inside me are so confused that in order to stay sane, I desperately begin to seek an understanding of what happened. Why did this happen to such a wonderful person? Other taxi drivers were angry when Mr. T kept getting rides from foreigners, especially adoptive families and their acquaintances. Mr. T had managed to save some money. I stare at the wall. I feel guilty about our friendship and our relationship of trust. Guilt is endlessly consuming. I have only meant well, but now I realize that cooperation with one can be a disservice to others if it does not help the whole community. I remember the moments in Kenya. I sometimes saw a bruise on Mr. T's face. When I asked about it, I got a belittling answer. Should I have foreseen what was coming? And could I have done something differently?

I won't ever know that. Now there is only guilt and sadness.

Mr. T's death taught me in a harsh way how important it is in relief work to ensure help for the whole community, so that everyone benefits from the help that comes to one. For example, Plan works well in this matter. With its godfather activities, it helps the whole community instead of one child. In this way, no child rises to an unequal position compared to others. I'm trying to think that I wasn't in Kenya doing aid work. Neither I nor anyone else in Mr. T's family could have imagined what our cooperation and friendship would lead to. And I will never find out if there was anything I could have done differently to prevent the situation from escalating to his death.

I thought about how we could help Mr T's children and widow. One adoptive mother says that the Finnish congregation could organize a collection. We participate in the collection, but nothing will bring Mr. T back. He had dreams and goals, which we often talked about. I advised and helped him on our long journeys together. He would have deserved all the good that the world has to offer. Mr. T did everything for us that we needed. We thought we did the same for him.

Life is not fair. Things happen whether we like it or not. We can't control everything. In order to try to move on I try to forget what happened. I have to be able to continue living and keep my focus on my children. I also need to focus at work, because our next children are probably already waiting somewhere in the world. We just don't know where yet.

Violence comes close again when we hear about an explosion in a familiar shopping center. There has been an armed attack on the Westgate shopping center in Nairobi. Hearing that makes us pause. Westgate is one of the most popular places to stay for adoptive families staying in Nairobi. We used to go there often. After a three-day siege, 67 people have died and 175 have been wounded. The attack crosses the news threshold in Finland in September 2013, three years after our return. We watch the news footage from the scene in disbelief. I remember the feelings that avoidance of the blow in Myyrmanni evoked. What if I had been in Westgate with my family when the attack happened? During our stay in Nairobi, there was no indication that the shopping center in question could be the target of an attack by extremist groups. Terrorism, as its name implies, sows fear even in those who are not directly targeted by terrorist acts. I feel bad for the victims and their loved ones. There is still so much to improve in the world.

I I I

"A child's life is like a piece of paper on which each person leaves a mark"
Chinese proverb [10]

Before meeting his adoptive parents, the adopted child has had various encounters and experiences that have left their mark on him. Our job as adoptive parents to read these signs to better understand our child.

Clover

After the procedure, I wake up in the hall to the nurse's voice: - Wake up and try to say something on the phone. I can hold the phone. This is your daughter, Melissa, she has been crying all night, afraid of losing you. After the call, I stay awake for a while and think that luckily Melissa has been able to experience a lot of good moments with us, even though now she has to experience another shock again. My thoughts blur and sleep wins and takes me back to Melissa and Topias' childhood.

Crash. After coming from Kenya, I am moving from my Africa projects to another employer, to the IT sector again. At work, I am writing a large public procurement offer in a hurry, the deadline for submission is at hand. I'm still reading and researching the last round of revisions to make sure all the areas worked on by the different experts are included. Suddenly the phone rang. I wonder why my father might be calling me at work at this time? I answer quickly: - I'm in a hurry, is there an emergency?

My father exclaims: - Yes, it's an emergency, Petri has had an accident with the children, you must come immediately! Everyone is alive, but you need to come here.

I'm completely shocked. My manager notices the situation and asks what's wrong. After telling him about it, he tells that I must to go to the crash site immediately. I'm lucky, because I've always had such warm-hearted bosses.

- Who will finish the offer and takes care of submitting it? I ask in shock.

- Now don't worry about it, we'll be taken care of, now just leave quickly. He says.

I decide to order a taxi because I don't dare to drive in a panic.

The taxi comes quickly and takes me to the crash site. Topias complains of pain in the chest and Melissa in her hip. The seat belt in the seat had hurt Topias in a sudden collision. Melissa's little legs were straight forward in the seat, having been pinched when the front seat came in with the front of the car. The car is absolutely crushed and is going to be redeemed. The situation would have had the ingredients for a much more serious crash. The woman driving the other car hadn't seen our small family car coming behind the big minivan when she was driving and blinded by the sun as she turned in front. The woman is crying, she too has been startled by the accident. Everyone's life had once again come too close to be lost. My fear of losing grows even more, just when it had eased after Topias and Melissa came home.

I decide to perk up and turn my eyes towards the future, from dark thoughts to light. Our dream of four children lives on. The adoption process has started again. We will find out where in the world we could get a little brother or little sister for Topias and Melissa with a short waiting time. We are no longer ready to go to Kenya because the trip was so eventful and some parts scary for us.

Adoption counselling is short compared to Kenya adoption. In Kenya, we had already learned that we don't adopt alone, we adopt as a family. Topias had already wisely told the representatives of the adoption organization before the trip to Kenya that we would adopt Melissa. He also adopted and not just us parents. We hope that the age difference between the children will not be too big. I hear about China's Special Needs program, which works well. Especially children with cleft lip and palate come to Finland from there, and waiting times are short. Since Finland has one of the best treatments in the world for these children, this seems like the most potential option. We also learned that compared to the population, Finland has the most cleft palates in the world.

In the Special Needs process, we need to choose and tick on the form which health restrictions we would be willing to accept for our future child. It has always been important for us as a family to move together in nature, and at the same time we as a family must be able to meet the special needs of the child. At first, we think that in this situation we would not be able to adopt a child with, for example, a visual impairment. Then our family would be split in two, with one parent staying with the child while the other left for the forest. On the other hand, nowadays Finland is already barrier-free in many places

135

and choosing these routes would be successful. We try to make choices about the child's health considering both perspectives. The most important thing would be that the child does not have any illness that could cause us to lose him. It would be too violent an experience for the whole family. After careful consideration, we decide to join the Special Needs program in China. We would have a child from China!

Life rolls on its own weight while we are waiting news of our new child. At work and at home, everyday life rolls on while we wait for information about the child. It's early Monday morning and time is not even seven o'clock yet. I go to work early in the dark of the morning, because I want to be on time to put everything in order before the clients arrive for the training. I walk into the office. Through the creaking wooden stairs and the glass door, I reach the corridor, which meanders in the morning twilight towards the classroom at the other end of the building. With the automatic lights coming on behind me, I hurried down the narrow corridor towards the training class. However, when I see the restaurant hall on the way, I stop in the corridor. I suddenly feel cold air, even though the restaurant has always been warm and cozy. Even though I'm indoors, I notice the scent of the bushes outside the building is strong. In the gloom I see that the front door is closed. Where does this cold draft of the morning dew come in? I carefully enter the restaurant hall opening from the corridor and see only darkness in front of me. Before I can wonder why the lights don't come on, I realize I'm standing in a sea of glass. Shards of glass sink into the soles of my shoes. It's been broken into! The window is broken. As horror gripped me, I wondered if the perpetrators were still here. Terror fills me when I realise the intruder or several of them could be watching me right now from the darkness. Instinct turns me around and I find myself running down the narrow corridor back towards the open office wing. If only someone were here. In the distance, I notice the lights of the screen reflecting off the face of one of my colleagues from the darkness. – Can you help me? Someone has broken in here. Let's call the cops! I scream and my male colleague rushes to help. The cops will be here soon. The police check the premises and find that the burglars knew what they had come to get, and that they had already left in the darkness of the night hours before.

After what happened, I reflected on my fears. How different it is in different situations and how the body reacts to it in different ways. Fear at the time of miscarriage is mentally and physically excruciating. Fear after Topias was born, when the harlequin effect came, it was as if someone slapped consciousness on a canvas. The fear at the police station was foggy, both the situation itself and the fear of losing my child and my own life pounding in my head. Fear with Topias and Mr. T in the taxi to the hospital was a panicked and overactive attempt to resolve the situation. When I got to the crash site, the uncertainty made it difficult to breathe. The fear of loss has been common in everything. Some events have had in common the fear of what will happen next. A feeling where all senses are attuned to a physical escape. I felt that fear in fast-forward after seeing the break-in.

A four-leaf clover is like winning the lottery. Again. The whole family is at a children's event in the yard of an old stone house on a hill near our home. We look for four-leaf clovers with children from other families in the clover meadow. Surprisingly, we find a four-leaf clover! That's enough joy and amazement for everyone. The search accelerates when the other children also want to find the four-leaf clover. Suddenly we find another four-leaf clover. The amazement is great. Statistically, about every ten thousand clovers is a four-leaf clover, and we found two in no time. The father of one family laughs that there are so many lucky ingredients in the air that we will definitely win next Saturday's lottery draw.

The next morning the phone rang. The Save the Children association is calling to tell us that a little 3.5-year-old boy is waiting for us in China. This is our family's lottery win! Oh, the joy when we tell the future big brother and big sister about it. We immediately leave for the association's office to get the child's information.

We have decided on names for a boy and a girl. If the child is a boy, he would be Elias, a combination of the names Topias and Melissa. Our hearts melt when we see his happy charming smile in the picture as he bustles about in the big playroom of the children's home. The orphanage has 1300 children, so it is huge compared to Melissa's small orphanage. If only we could get on our way soon and see your captivating smile, our dear child! There is still a lot to do before then. We go through Elias' papers with a doctor to know what we should prepare for. Elias has a bilateral cleft lip and palate, which would require several surgeries. Otherwise, the boy is healthy and well. Nothing life-threatening is known. The most important thing is to get Elias home safely. We will get through everything that comes our way, just like before.

Beijing, China. In 2012, approximately 17 million people live in Beijing. A decade later, the city has wedged itself into the world's ten largest cities with a population of more than 20 million.

We are leaving for China with my parents, who have travelled in China before. Fortunately, they help us when Melissa and Topias are excited and in a busy mood. In crowded subways in a foreign country, it is important that there are more of us adults and that everyone understands that it is not a holiday. Based on the lessons we learned from Kenya, we know that anything can happen. It takes courage and confidence that we can get through everything. With cooperation, flexibility and quick response. In advance, the trip feels short compared to the previous one.

We would only be in China for three weeks, because everything is already thought out. There would be a lot of traveling in a short time. Otherwise, the arrival of a new family member always takes strength, even if it is a happy event. Even though everything in China is very pre-planned and scheduled, we certainly wouldn't avoid surprises there either.

There are four families of us in the same group at the same time. All have big brothers for future little brothers. In addition to our big brother, we also have big sister Melissa with us. We all stay in the same hotel. My parents' and our rooms are connected by an intermediate door, so we can relax in the room without fear of the children getting lost in the elevator by themselves.

Our local guide is an experienced guide of Finnish adoptive families. He is a relaxed, friendly and funny man. The ponytail just swings as he runs errands and resolves situations. In the lobby of the hotel, while we are waiting for other families for the first joint program of the day, he lifts Melissa up to the reception desk and makes everyone laugh as Melissa waves to the others from high up. He wonders and admires Melissa's skin, not its colour, but its softness. He marvels that Melissa's skin feels like the most expensive Chinese silk. How can someone's skin be like this? Melissa is happy and the guide makes her a good friend right away. All the children also want to try Melissa's skin. I myself only now realize how unique it is. Just like all our children, each of them is unique, a master drawing.

Diamond

We are getting used to the new country for a few days before we leave Beijing together with other families for Taijuan, where our adopted children would join us. On the first day, our guide takes us shopping on the subway. When we step into Walmart, it becomes clear that China (or at least Beijing) is not quite as exotic as we had expected. Visits to McDonald's, Pizza Hut, KFC and Starbucks confirm this notion. On our trip, we luckily get to explore more local culinary experiences under the guidance of our guide, but unfortunately often when moving around by ourselves, ordering food from menus in Chinese still feels like too exotic a challenge.

The journey of almost 600 kilometres to Taiyan last almost 3 hours with bullet train. Looking out of the window we see signs of China's rapid growth and urbanization all around us. In every city we pass, several skyscrapers are currently being built.

Taijuan is one of the hometowns of the Chinese space program. The roofs of many tall buildings are decorated with a shape resembling a space rocket and decorative dishes and antennas pointing into space. We would have more time to admire these extraordinary buildings next week, when we would get used to life as a family with three children.

Today is a big day, today is the day we will meet Elias, or Gugu actually. Children in China are often called by the last syllable of their name, saying it twice. So, we also call him Gugu when we meet.

Gugu has been brought from his hometown to Taijuan, where the agency responsible for adoption in the region is located. We arrive at the large lobby of the agency and are told to sit on the sofas. Petri paces back and forth nervously, until he suddenly stops and looks towards the large glass doors of the office: - it looks like someone familiar is coming this way now.

We all turn to look in the direction where a small, brisk boy steps from the other end of the hall, hand firmly in his nurse's hand. We recognized him immediately from the pictures sent to us: in front of us is our beloved son. He smiles but looks thoughtful. He doesn't fully understand what is happening. At the orphanage, he has been shown the photos we sent and told who we are. We carefully take a couple of steps closer to them. Then Gugu suddenly releases his grip on the nurse and runs straight into Petri's arms, who is squatting on the floor. The moment is really moving and happy. This boy now has gotten his family! We adore Gugu and his smile. He smiles widely at the world and knows that this is his place, in his father's arms.

After a while, I too have sunny Gugu in my arms and he grabs me by my braids, just like Melissa did a few years ago in Kenya. I notice that the nurse who brought Gugu also has braids like me. It had been safe to hold onto it and make sure to get the nurse's attention and closeness. The situation is also moving for the nurse because she is now escorting the little one to his new home. She has taken care of Gugu for a long time in the children's home and joined Gugu on his long car trip here.

Topias and Melissa have a red lollipop that they give to Gugu. Gugu can't seem to stay inside his oversized yellow coat with a monkey pattern as he excitedly opens his lollipop with the help of his sister and brother. The smell of caramel is wafting in the air. Gugu knows, in addition to the sugary taste pleasure that will soon begin, that these two children wish him well. He belongs among them.

Gugu has a yellow coat and we too have been instructed to wear red and yellow, colours that mean good luck in China. In the office, we move to another room where the official papers are made. Another foreign family is rejoicing there with their adopted child. Some Finnish families received a hand-painted scroll, we are handed a red folder embroidered with golden letters from the orphanage, inside which our name and Chinese text are embroidered on folded paper.

At the hotel, Gugu walks happily in our room and already dares to peek through the intermediate door to the grandparents' room. Soon he is already running between rooms. Gugu gets excited to play Muppet Rally in Topias' arms on the same portable PlayStation that was Topias's joy a few years earlier in Kenya. Gugu also happily plays with toys with Melissa. We have learned twenty words and phrases in Chinese so that we can instruct Gugu. In the evening, he falls asleep easily when his sister and brother are close to him, holding his big brother's hand. This adopted child also feels safer with other children, like Melissa in her time. It is good that there are groups on adoption trips. In this way, even the children who are adopted into the family that doesn't have other children can feel that they are receiving protection from other kids after a big change has taken place in the beginning of their new phase of life.

The first times we move around the city, Gugu's walking style catches my attention. He holds onto Petri's hand tightly with one hand and the other hand even goes back in rhythm with the step of the feet as if marching. His gaze is firmly forward. Gugu doesn't even glance at Topias or Melissa, who are jumping here and there on the sidewalk. I realize that the boy is acting exactly as he has been taught. He's not even four years old yet. I'm trying to show Gugu that he can walk the way he wants. He is amazed and does not understand. I show that he can walk on the sidewalk sometimes next to me and sometimes with Melissa and Topias. He carefully releases his grip on Petri's hand and walks at his own pace, following our reactions. We are all smiling and Gugu is giddy with joy. He walks from person to person. Some point, he grabs both of our hands, swings himself hanging from our hands, and with our help, he takes big leaps forward. Gugu laughs and couldn't be happier.

In Kenya, Melissa's citizenship was already confirmed in Nairobi and she received a Finnish passport from the embassy for travel. Adopted children from China travel to Finland as Chinese citizens with a Chinese passport. We would get Gugu's passport from the office in his hometown. The other families stay in Taijuan and we continue our journey several hours by car away from the big city. There we also could visit Gugu's orphanage. On the car trip, we see the Great Wall of China for the first time, which winds along the high, steep mountain slopes. Gugu's hometown was once an important garrison town, the northernmost outpost of this part of the wall. We follow the progress of the wall in the mountains for a large part of our long car journey.

The orphanage is large and consists of several large multi-storey grey buildings. From many windows we see small faces wondering at strange-looking guests. We get to see rooms where children have activities according to different topics: gymnastics, learning letters and reading, rehabilitation for those who need it, a playground and so on. Everything is very organized, and the children walk in completely straight lines from one point to another, just like in Guguk's first days in Taijuan. Outside, children walk in bullet-straight lines. I especially remember the smiling girl standing in one of the queues. The girl is very badly burned all over, especially on the face. I wish that hopefully a family will be found for her soon. Fortunately, she is receiving treatment here.

"A diamond with a crack is better than a normal stone that is perfect"
Chinese proverb [11]

Children with cleft palate, like others, can have abnormalities in appearance. There are many different-looking children in the orphanage, all equally sweet. According to a Chinese proverb, I wish that all people would always pay attention to the person instead of the appearance and want to get to know him.

We sleep one night in a hotel near the orphanage. We won't have time to get to explore the city in more detail, after visiting the orphanage and getting Gugu's passport from the agency, we will be taken back to Taijuan. When we leave, we cross the river and look at the big dragon statue behind us from the bridge. Petri remembers having read somewhere that in Chinese mythology, dragons originated from dinosaur fossils that are abundant in China.

When we were in Taijuan, it was still one of the ten most polluted cities in the world. Since then, to improve the situation, the city has ordered a ban on coal burning in certain areas and developed energy infrastructure. In Beijing we had seen all kinds of plastic toys and stuff. Gugu had taken his most beloved toy from the children's home, a plastic crawling baby that shook its head, cried and played loud disco music. The toy was almost completely played with and soon it fell apart. Gugu had presented the toy to his siblings and the children agree that a new one must be obtained. Despite the fun of the toy, it felt pointless. We had seen similar products of similar quality on sale in Kenyan markets. I wonder how much the environment is destroyed in making and transporting all of them from here on the other side of the world to our north and elsewhere around the world. An endless amount of products on the shelves of Finnish stores says "Made in China". Together with the children, we decide not to buy a new toy, but to fix the broken baby toy after we return to Finland.

After returning to Beijing, our family still has almost two weeks before returning home. Time is spent, among other things, to confirm the adoption at the embassy and to obtain the necessary visa and other documents for the new family member. While waiting for the documentaries, we spend time sightseeing. Our guide will lead us and other Finnish adoptive families to get to know the destinations we requested in advance. At the top of the list is the Great Wall of China. According to Chinese belief, a boy becomes a man only after walking on the Great Wall of China, so according to our guide, every Chinese boy in our group had to step on it. The claim known from Chinese textbooks about the Great Wall of China being the only man-made structure visible from space is not true. Nevertheless, the Great Wall of China is a mind-numbing experience. The Great Wall of China is actually not one wall but several, dating back to 200 BC. - After 1600, a defence structure consisting of a part built during the beginning of the era. Due to the long construction history, the length of the wall is stated to be from 6,000 kilometres to more than 21,000 kilometres, but usually no more than 9,000 kilometres. It is mostly a wall about eight meters high built of earth, stone and brick, shaping the contours of the terrain. Our guide takes us to a part of the wall in Mutianyu that was completed in the middle of the 16th century. It is located about 70 kilometers northwest of Beijing. In a destination normally bursting with tourists, on a chilly October-November morning, there were only a handful of other tourists in addition to us. Of course, a handful of people in China is many times more than what a handful means in Finland. The wall itself is stunningly beautiful and that part of the wall is one of the best preserved. My star moment is when I get to take the photo I've been dreaming of for a long time on the wall. In it, Topias and Melissa are standing on the wall with their hands in the hands of the little brother standing in the middle of them, looking at the winding of the wall disappearing into the distance in the mountains that open before us.

Gugu already clearly trusts us more and lets us take care of him more and more. In the beginning, we were only able to quickly change the diaper. After returning from the windy and cold Great Wall of China, we decide to try a bath. Petri runs warm bath water for the children in our hotel room. Melissa and Topias jump into the tub habitually and Gugu carefully follow. The children fool around with the bath foam and Gugu gets excited to join in the game. Petri has bought a Chinese flag as a souvenir earlier in the day. He comes to the bathroom to show the flag he bought. When Gugu sees the flag, he jumps up in the tub to stand with his back straight and starts clapping with a big smile in honour of the flag. This is how he has been taught at the orphanage and it makes us smile. I take out the towel and drain the water from the tub. Melissa and Topias shower first and leave the bathroom. I gently spray Gugu and notice something strange on his lower back. I immediately get a lump in my throat. I remember reading that a change like this in a child can be potentially life-threatening. I try my best to hide my panic from Gugu and ask Petri and my parents to be there. We need our guide here fast. Fear overwhelms me, but I act like a robot. Fortunately, the guide is at the hotel, and he quickly comes to our room. I say what I suspect, and he looks at Gugu's back. He is sure we have nothing to worry about. He has seen one of the sad cases I suspect in question diagnosed and this one doesn't look like that at all. We are relieved and grateful to the guide. Dear little Gugu will survive. I tuck the kids to sleep. With them safely asleep, my fear of losing Gugu erupts in uncontrollable sobs into my pillow.

Our next destination is the Forbidden City. The former residence of Chinese emperors is now one of Beijing's central attractions. As the name of the palace indicates, most subjects were forbidden to enter the palace and only the emperor was allowed to move freely in the area. We are approaching the Forbidden City from the Tiananmen Square. Above the gate leading to the palace is a large picture of Mao Zedong, the founder of the People's Republic of China. We come through a big and high entrance to a big open place like an arena. It's funny that when Petri admires and photographs a wonderful place, all the Chinese people swarming around take pictures of Petri, who has a sweet African girl on his back. As a great lover of history, Petri tries to absorb everything possible from the incredible palace, while smiling Chinese people occasionally approach him, asking Petri and Melissa to take a picture with them. I photograph Petri from the side, holding back my laughter, Petri gives permission to photograph with friendly nod for more and more new people who ask for permission to photograph. Petri is smiling. We are in one of the most famous attractions in the world and everyone wants to photograph Petri and Melissa instead, because they are celebrities here.

After the tour, our guide will take us to eat from the area of the main street with international restaurant chains to a side alley that

146

opens the lives of the locals. It's peaceful compared to the hustle and bustle of the Forbidden City. There is a small barbershop, car maintenance and other services along the alley. The guide leads us into a small restaurant. We don't stay at the tables but are guided through the door at the back of the restaurant to the bedroom, the waiters put the double bed on the wall and the room turns into a cabinet in no time. We all sit together in a tight circle around a large round table. We inquire about the possibility of washing hands before eating. There is no toilet in the restaurant, so we are directed a short distance to the side of the street, where we can find the common toilet of this residential area. One serving dish after another comes to our table and our guide tells us which delicacies are brought to us at any given time. We eat with a good appetite after walking around the palace area for a couple of hours. Serving dishes circulate on the table. Everything tastes good, some even exotic. Another steaming serving dish is brought from the kitchen to the table. Petri turns to our guide: - Excuse me, what kind of meat is this food.

Our guide asks the waiter something in Chinese and is content to answer Petri's answer briefly: - Yes.

The contents of the food remain a mystery, but it looks and smells delicious, so the dish empties quickly as it goes around the table.

We travel a lot by subway in Beijing. It can be somewhat challenging. First, we need to check that our whole party is definitely on board. There are so many people getting cramped in the subway that everyone is completely squeezed to each other, and the doors can't be closed. In Finland, there is no such crowd even in the most popular discount sales. There really isn't a any of space between people. Still, everyone remains calm. When I get up on my toes, all I see is people's dark hair and Petri's head rising from among the people and Melissa on her back. Gugu is on my back, and I hold Topias's hand tightly and press him against me. When we get our whole family, including my non-English speaking parents, out of the subway at the right stop while people are rushing in, we can say that the adventure was a success. Petri is laughing. In Helsinki, the metro used to feel crowded if each passenger didn't have his own seat. The metro in Helsinki is actually pretty empty even in the worst rush hour.

When visiting China, of course you must go see pandas as well. They can be seen at the Beijing Zoo. All pandas living in zoos around the world are the property of China. China practices the so-called panda diplomacy by renting animals. In few years, a couple of pandas would be leased to the zoo in Finland.

Our guide is also helpful in the zoo. He gets along very well with Gugu and they walk hand in hand admiring the animals. He tells Gugu in Chinese about the animals we saw. We have time to help Melissa and Topias and tell them about animals in Finnish.

We walk a lot in the city and in nearby parks. Everywhere is clean and moving around feels safe. The air feels fresh enough, only one day walking outside in Beijing the air stings eyes and throat. Due to the smog, you can't see the skyscrapers on the other side of the highway that goes in front of the hotel. I thought about what direction the air pollution will develop in the coming years.

Time in Beijing passes quickly. It's wonderful to just spend time with family without rushing anywhere. The "do only one thing a day" we learned in Kenya works well in China as well. We take small walks, marvel at the towering buildings around us and rest. Finally, the day comes when we get the necessary documents for our journey home from the embassy. We pack our suitcases and do one last round of shopping. Our guide takes us to the adjacent silk market for shopping and guides us in haggling. According to him, it is not worth paying more than two euros for a nice shirt that costs 20 euros in Europe.

At the airport, our guide says a warm goodbye to our children and our journey continues towards Finland. He gives them little memories of the trip and finally gets down in front of Gugu. He puts his hands on Gugu's shoulders and says something quietly to him in Chinese. Maybe he gives some life advice or encouragement to the little person as he goes out into the world. We will never know what it was, it will remain between them. Our guide stands up and turns in our direction with wet eyes and states that Gugu is growing into a fine boy. The emotional farewell is over quickly. Now I focus intently on guiding our party through the large airport to the blue and white plane. It will transport our family, which has grown with one child, home to Finland.

We will hold the christening in the same stone house on the hill where we had found two four-leaf clovers months before. Although Gugu is officially christened Elias, the original name given in China becomes his official middle name. The name Gugu will remain in use as a nickname. Later, two other boys named Elias join the same class at school. The teacher asks that Elias could be called Gugu at school too, and that suits the boy and us.

Cardiac ambulance

Gugu adapts to our family naturally. Weekly speech therapy, monthly orthodontic treatments and various surgeries now and then will be a new thing in our everyday life. Other than that, life with our three children is very normal.

The "headquarters" under his bed is important to Gugu. It is the area under the bed, where the children can reach from end of the bed through the door built by Petri. The lemurs are also important, we go to see them while on vacation in Spain at Fuengirola Zoo. It's funny when Gugu and his friends often hide under his bed and the lemur plush toy is involved in the play. As a lively boy, Gugu makes a lot of friends quickly, even though his speech is still unclear before all the surgeries are finished and the Finnish language is difficult.

Gugu loves Legos more than anything, just like his brother Topias when he was small. Gugu is really looking forward to his surgeries because we promise to get him the Lego package, he wants in advance so he can build it right after he recovers from the surgery.

Soon after returning to Finland, we are referred as a client to a unit specialized in the treatment of cleft lip and palate, in Helsinki. We are told that the treatment will progress like a train from that moment until Gugu's adulthood. I would like to see this kind of professionalism, planning and friendliness in all healthcare in the world. All the doctors, nurses and therapists treating Gugu know the patient and parents do not have to explain the child's medical history every time. Petri states that he now understands the benefit of the "family doctor" that we have seen in American television series. It is really easy when one doctor is responsible for the overall treatment, who, if necessary, consults professionals from other specialties.

The change in Gugu's back that I noticed in Beijing will be confirmed as harmless at the Children's Clinic and will be treated. I'm slowly starting to be calmer while waiting for diagnoses. Maybe you don't always have to fear the worst, and I'll try to think "healthy until proven otherwise" in the future. This is not easy, but little by little I am learning that there is a solution to every situation if you just look for it.

The day of surgery finally arrives. A palate would be built for Gugu first. Of course, we knew what we were getting into when we were ready to adopt a cleft palate patient as our child. But still, It must have been a bit of a surprise for Petri, when he first looked into Gugu's mouth and actually saw that the palate was missing, or when Gugu was eating, some of the food could come out through the nose. I am reasonably calm before surgery. It should be pretty much a routine procedure for the top team. Fortunately, Finland has such a high level of expertise in these surgeries that even in the face of unexpected situations, the staff is able to act to save the child.

When I arrived at the hospital, I heard that the surgery would take about a couple of hours. I'm alone in Gugu's room waiting. I open my laptop and start working during the surgery. Working helps me forget the hospital worries for a while as I focus on nice client projects. I startle when I see the nurse peeking through the window of the door. I look at the clock and notice that almost three hours have already passed. I don't worry, because the nurse smiles at me. Is there something in his smile, though, with concern? He says hello and continues his way. I think everything is definitely fine, I immerse myself in my work again. Suddenly the door opens. The operating doctor comes straight to me from the salon. I glance at the clock on the wall. An hour has passed since the nurse's greeting. The doctor says that the structure of Gugu's face is very unusual and at some point, the situation was getting serious. Everything is fine now. The surgeon says that many of the most difficult operations in this field of medicine, in the world are performed in Finland. According to him, Gugu's surgery will make it to the Top5. As a professional and as a person, the surgeon is in a class of his own, such a great guy! Fortunately, he will be in Gugu's life for a long time and will also perform the following operations.

Gugu wakes up groggy, but immediately remembers Legos and tries to sit up to start playing. I help a large Lego package to the bed next to him. Gugu is happy trying to open the package and to connect two Legos without success. I explain that the anaesthetic is still working. He manages to build then when the substance leaves the body. Gugu falls asleep tired with his legos and lemur.

We get home on Saturday morning. I try to feed Gugu yogurt. He keeps his mouth tightly shut. He should eat at least a little, but his mouth remains resolutely shut. Finally, I tell Gugu to open his mouth to see if everything is okay. As he opens his mouth, to my horror I notice that the newly built palate has fallen from one side onto the tongue. I'll call the hospital. The surgeon who operated on Gugu is just about to go on vacation abroad with his family. The nurse catches up with the surgeon, whose flight, luckily, hasn't left yet. Emergency surgery is needed immediately, and the surgeon jumps into a taxi.

We start driving towards the hospital as well. Gugu is quickly put to sleep and during surgery the palate is fixed in a new way. It had fallen because his mouth is an extraordinary shape. The surgeon's professionalism is commendable again even in this new situation. Gugu is urgently rushed from Töölö Hospital to the Children's Clinic. Petri follows Gugu to the door of the operating room and waits outside. At night, there is no waiting room in the hospital, so he walks outside in the freezing cold around the area during the surgery. After a couple of hours, the news comes that the surgery has ended successfully and Gugu will be transferred back to Töölö Hospital. Petri could stay overnight in the little patient's room.

Gugu starts kindergarten. He makes friends there too. One day when I come to pick up Gugu, he enthusiastically tells me what has happened during the day. I can't understand anything. I ask him to speak a little slower so I can understand better. The little boy standing next to Gugu looks at me confused. He thinks I'm a bit stupid and states that Gugu speaks perfectly clear. I smile at him. This is how it is that children understand each other completely when they spend their days together.

Gugu starts second grade at the same elementary school where his older siblings also go to school. It's Finland's Independence Day and Finland turns 100 years old today. There is a festive flag-raising ceremony at the school. Gugu has recovered well from the flu that plagued him earlier, but just in case, I've kept him at home for a few more days of recuperation. I've been working remotely to make sure he's fine before going back to school. As usual, Gugu quickly slips out the front door and is walking in the direction of school with his cousin before I know it. The weather is cold. I didn't realize to offer them a ride. I'm sure the boys will make it, I think care free and head to the workplace. My workday barely starts when I get a call from school. Gugu is lying in the school nurse's room and the ambulance is coming.

Melissa told me that after the flag has been gotten to pole in the morning, the intermission started right away. The children were playing in the freezing cold. Gugu had come to Melissa and complained about the heart. A cardiac ambulance had been called to the school. I quickly jump into the car and head towards the school hill. Every red light in traffic is too much. It feels like a familiar dark figure is throwing blocks in the way so that I don't make it in time to help save my child. Will Gugu survive?

When I arrive at school, I see Gugu being lifted into the ambulance. I rush to him and jump into the ambulance next to him. Melissa is scared and joins the front seat. The ambulance sets off quickly. It is stated that the values predicting a heart attack are clearly elevated, but help has been there in time. Before this, the heart had not given any signs of possible problems, not even when Gugu was on the operating table. In the children's hospital's heart clinic, studies show that mutations can also be found elsewhere in the body in addition to the mouth area. With Gugu, the mutation is found in the heart. He is missing a flap and the second flap has grown to the third. Fortunately, the defect was found so that the heart can be protected in the following surgeries. We are grateful that his heart has survived the previous operations without protection. Everything happens so fast that I don't understand what is happening. With fear in the background, I mechanically absorb information from the doctors and help Gugu as best I can. However, the situation is not acute and there is no need to do anything about it right now. We get home and wait for the invitation to the follow-up visit in the mail.

Some months later, I'm in work meeting and I see a text message from Gugu. It has a broken heart. Gugu has sent emojis of different emotional states before, so in that situation I didn't worry about it. Besides, Gugu will surely be in touch with Petri too if he has something important. After a while, I notice that Melissa has made many calls to me. At the same time, the phone starts vibrating as Melissa chases after me again. I apologize to the other meeting participants and go into the corridor to answer the call: - Mother is in the meeting, is there an emergency? I ask as I have so many times before when the children call in the middle of the workday.
- Gugu is lying here in front of the school, it's his heart again, we need help. Melissa screams into the phone in a panic.
I startle, but my fear immediately subsides when I start instructing Melissa like a machine: - Immediately find an adult and tell them that it's a heart problem. See that someone is with Gugu. Call the ambulance, 112. Soon I will be with Melissa again by Gugu's hospital bed. Petri also arrives shortly in the room panting and sits breathlessly on the chair next to the boy. He hadn't realised to react to the broken heart emoji he'd received either. We realize together how clever Gugu had been in trying to communicate the situation to his parents. We decide among the whole family that if Gugu sends a broken heart emoji, then it's real emergency. Otherwise, broken heart emoji should not be used.

For a couple of years, the heart does not cause problems. Gugu is healthy and even starts trampoline gymnastics as a trainee in a competition group. Perhaps good muscle condition and the fact that Gugu, as a busy little man, always runs everywhere, supports heart health as well. However, in the fall of the fourth grade, I get a call from Gugu's teacher. Gugu has been swimming with the class. As a competitive spirit, he has swum a long distance at high speed with his friends. His heart begins to sting again. His friend notices that his strength is weakening and helps Gugu to the edge of the pool. Luckily, the teacher knows about Gugu's situation and calls the cardiac ambulance. I wouldn't be able to get to the swimming hall before the ambulance leaves, so I head straight to the New Children's Hospital. This time too, we'll survive with a scare. Gugu has remained positive throughout the journey, as have we. Together we will get through this too. We are sad for him about his health situation, but happy that the boy is enjoying his life despite the heart problems.

Hospital clown

The message we were waiting for comes from the hospital: Gugu's facial bones would be ready for the construction of the upper jaw. The jaw bones could be transplanted to the face from the iliac bones of the hip. The doctors are preparing for surgery. The surgical team also includes an anaesthesiologist specializing in heart defects, so all risks should be considered. Our relatives, friends and work community are strongly involved in the spirit. Gugu has already changed on to his surgical clothes and I am waiting with him for the surgery to start. I am very nervous, but Gugu doesn't find the operation scary at all. He couldn't bear to wait and impatiently asks when he will be picked up. A funny hospital clown enters the room. Hospital clowns make children and us adults forget their illness for a while and give mental permission for a good mood, liberating laughter and madness in the middle of everyday hospital life. Hospital clowns are art professionals who have been trained to work in a demanding hospital environment.

Hospital clowning started in the United States in the 1980s. It arrived in Finland in 2002. I have not met hospital clowns before. Elias is a little cautious at first but relaxes in no time. I am grateful for this small relief from the tension caused by the surgery. Time passes faster in the presence of a clown. He plays a little barrel organ and Gugu smiles.

The nurse comes to us and releases the brakes on Gugu's bed. Gugu wants the clown to go with us. He plays the radio and sings all the way to the operating room. Gugu laughs and our sunny procession delights all the patients, doctors and other people we meet in the corridors. The doors to the operating room open and Gugu is pushed in with a smile. The clown says that he can go to the operating room with him. Gugu finds this a comforting thought, and the clown puts on protective clothing. Medicines flow into the veins and the smile behind Gugu's oxygen mask turns into a restful sleep. I hold back my tears and walk away. I'm very scared now. Hours pass before the doctor calls from the ward to say that everything is fine. Gugu's heart took the surgery just fine. I'll see your happy smile again soon.

The surgery recovery time is said to be a month of home care and even after that there are restrictions on exercise for a couple of months. Petri takes a month's unpaid leave from work and stays to take care of Gugu. For the first two days, Gugu hurts and complains about his hip and mouth. On the morning of the third day, he excitedly jumps out of bed when the pain is almost over. Petri has to come up with something calm to do with Gugu, so that he doesn't try to run around the apartment and possibly hurt himself. Children's ability to heal is incredible.

Gugu has been operated on a lot over the years. Fortunately, he has not developed any fear, in fact he feels the opposite. Gugu admires his operating doctor. The doctor says that many children who are treated a lot in the hospital either grow up avoiding hospitals or tend to work in the healthcare field. Gugu is clearly the latter. The American family doctor model mentioned by Petri has been critically important, especially for Gugu. He has had treatment teams made up of the same doctors all along. They know the patient as a whole and don't fumble the child in different places. Sometimes they have tried to refer us to a local health centre or emergency room or dental care in our area, until they realized that this top team is needed to take care of Gugu.

Car accident. After Gugu has recovered, we are on our way home from the shopping center with Melissa and Gugu. There is a huge downpour. Suddenly I notice a car in front of us stopped in the lane leading to the freeway ramp. I wondered with concern whether the driver had a seizure. I park our car behind the stopped car and run to the other one. The driver is fine and says that the car is completely stuck for no reason and they are just trying to call for help. At the same time, I notice a taxi speeding up from behind, trying to pass us, ignoring our stopped cars. The taxi drives towards Melissa and Gugu! I run as if in a dream to my car and see the scared but fortunately conscious children in the back seat.

The taxi driver gets out of the car yelling at me and blaming me for the damage to his car. I'll call the police. They arrive quickly. A female person from the car in front of us tells me that I stopped to help them. The police tell the taxi driver that it was already the scene of an accident, in which case everyone else is obliged to avoid it. The taxi is clearly to blame for the crash. Although stopping the car and helping was the right thing to do, my children's lives were at risk. It takes the sharpest edge out of my own impulsive desire to help other people in all situations. In the future, I will first consider the overall situation so that my loved ones are safe before helping others.

Looking at myself and my behaviour, I realize that as a mother I am very protective. So much has happened that I am constantly afraid that something bad will happen to our lively and active children. The children complain because I don't let them go to the beach without an adult, even though other children can go. I reflect the situation on my own experiences and fear that the sea current will take them away, like it happened to my friend's mother in Spain years before. Even in a place as safe as Finland's Westend beach, a lifeguard told me once that sometimes it's hard for him too to swim when the sea current pulls you upstream. So I'm like a hawk at the water's edge watching the kids, even though they think it's embarrassing. Relaxation in my motherhood in different situations develops little by little along with the growth of the children when the excitement matures into reasonableness.

Over time, each of our children begins to think more and more about where they came from and what it is like in the country of their birth. We start planning important root trips for them. Topias states that his roots go to Germany. We decide to be the first to fulfil our firstborn's travel wish. We travel to Germany via Legoland in Sweden and Denmark, so that the children can see our home from Topias' early childhood. Melissa doesn't want to travel to Kenya yet, the time would be later. Gugu is very interested in China and definitely wants to visit there. Adoption organizations organize customized root trips and we are planning one to China when Gugu turns ten. However, the trip moves into the future when the corona virus starts its world tour in the same year.

Children go to school and life settles down. Fanning a Finnish kid's heavy rock band Hevisaurus changes to Robin's songs, young pop star in Finland, the lyrics of many of which touch and give strength to us parents as well. It is privileged and at the same time so educational and full of work to grow up in parenthood with children. We are lucky that we get to be mother and father and family.

If everything falls apart and you need a shoulder
I promise to be here, for you, for you
And even if you don't always see me, I'm always here for you, for you
You will not be alone, you will not be alone [12]

ONLY STRAIGHT LINE

Luck and accident

The peaceful everyday life of a family with three children in my dream is interrupted when I feel someone touch my shoulder and I startle awake. I realize I'm still in the hospital and try to move, but a grimace spreads across my face. The friendly nurse says she will bring more painkillers. My strength is all gone. The nurse suggests a conversation with the priest. I agree because I don't know what else to do next. The nurse opens the door and the priest enters the room. He asks to tell about what happened. The priest says it can make me feel better. If I can't talk, we could just be together for a while. I begin to tell him about the fierce struggle to the death, from which I was the only one who survived. One of us didn't make it. The priest listens to the story. I lie down, look at the white ceiling and tell my story.

Our journey to family is not over yet. Our clover is awaiting its final fourth leaf.

We hope from the bottom of our hearts to experience childbirth and the baby period together with our children. So we get encouraged to try infertility treatments one more time. The treatments are tough again, but we are familiar with this, with its spikes, hormonal fog and everything, nothing surprises us. The ultimate cause of infertility is still obscure. When the cause has not been determined, anything is still possible. The infertility doctor we consulted encourages us to try, considering my age, pregnancy is still quite possible. We don't even have to think about it, we decide to try at least one more time.

The pregnancy starts well, like so many times before. Being wiser from previous experiences, we don't celebrate it, but let time pass and do frequent follow-ups. We don't tell the children anything, I rest a lot after work citing my stomach problems.

I feel like there are butterflies on the surface of my lower abdomen, tingling changes. Maybe soon I would feel movements. The children wonder why I don't go on the water slide at the water park, and I don't even dare to swim. I don't want to take any risk, even if the baby is safe. I am reading more information again. I eat, drink and act slavishly according to the instructions, just so that I wouldn't do anything wrong and that the baby is saved. I don't want to blame myself if everything goes wrong again. I blink to get rid of the horrible images of past miscarriages. Children do somersaults in the water. They excitedly talk about the wild turns in the tunnel of the water slide. I suggest eating ice cream and the whole laughing trio floats off the water. They join us at the table, blissfully unaware of the little brother in my belly.

The passing and critical twelve weeks have already been left behind. My uterus is in front, so my belly is already swollen. I wear loose clothes and complain of stomach problems and bloating.

Nobody knows to suspect anything, or at least doesn't say their doubts out loud. Many people think that pregnancy is not even possible for us. After all, we have two adopted children and getting Topias had been difficult.

We go for ultrasounds often and my belly is growing. One day, the doctor states that the pregnancy has progressed well and asks if I would like to take a look at the ultrasound now. I carefully turn to look, and our little darling is waving his arms and legs so excitedly that it feels like he is smiling and waving at us. Maybe soon I would caress your smile in my arms. Hope to see him soon, watching him to wave to us.

The doctor states that everything is looking great, the child is doing excellently and has grown completely normally. Everything had been fine in the NIPT test as well. We have a brisk, wonderful boy growing up. Petri and I had already talked that if a miracle happened and he was born, he would become Matias as a combination of our children's names. Second name would be Onni, which means happiness or luck in Finnish, as he completes our happiness.

When I walk out of the doctor's office, I'm happier than I've been in a long while. It is as if the evil cloud cover has finally lifted. The beautiful signs of spring add to my good spirits. I tell Petri that I finally have the courage to tell the children and everyone that the stomach swelling problem is the greatest luck. We will have a baby and our children will have a happy little brother. As long as we survive until the 25th week, he will survive. My former colleague's relative's baby also survived well that week, despite being born early.

After the children come home from school, we ask them to sit down and tell them that if everything goes well, they will have a little brother. They are amazed and excited and ask if they can tell everyone. We give permission. We call the future grandparents and inform relatives and friends. The evening is full of congratulations and joy. Gugu wants the children to write to Santa Claus on behalf of Matias now, so that the elves have time to make Matias' presents as well, because Matias will not be born until autumn. Then it's too late to write. And so they write to Santa even though it's spring. The joyful children go to sleep. Topias crawls under Gugu's table to make a playhouse for the night. The next day they would get to tell everyone the news at school.

The evening is already turning into night, but I can't sleep. I keep feeling like I need to go to the toilet, but nothing comes. I sit on the couch to read congratulatory messages on my phone. I feel uncomfortable. I get up and walk calmly in the living room to ease my stomach. I drink water and think about what I have eaten when my stomach plays tricks like this. I have been careful about my diet so that the pregnancy would progress well. A peculiar situation. I walk slowly towards the toilet again. Just before I get there, I feel like there is an explosion inside me. I can't stop the fact that in seconds the child is born as if baby is dropping from inside of me. I catch him and land on the floor. The child is lying next to me, and I am screaming for help. The blood comes with accelerating force, there is so much blood that I can barely stay conscious anymore. Petri runs to the scene, immediately calls an ambulance and uses another phone to alert my parents from the neighbour to help.

I'm lying in a pool of blood. With the last of my strength, I have lifted our little baby onto the towel. He's completely lifeless, but I'm trying to revive him. Petri is trying to make me understand reality. Shocked, he says the child is dead and focuses on getting me to the hospital. Petri is afraid of every minute. I'm going to die if help doesn't come soon. He calls the emergency phone many times and shouts; why the ambulance is taking so long. He is horrified by the profuse bleeding. The blood is already gushing out. My eyes get blurry and keep slide in and out of consciousness when I wake up and see figures around me. I hear the quiet sound from the door as the boys peek out of their rooms worried, sad and shocked. Everyone is just waiting for an ambulance. My mother tries to keep me awake by talking to me and my father puts coats from the hall as a cushion under my head on the bloody stone floor. I make out Melissa's figure in my field of vision. She talks quietly to herself as if someone has been murdered. The front door is open. I hear the sound of sirens. Outside, a blue flickering light is reflected in Petri's waving hands. The sirens are getting louder and closer. The ambulance stops, the paramedics arrive and kneel down to me and begin treating me quickly. I try to shout in a thin voice from the pool of blood that save the baby. I hold the little person in my arms carefully. Shock and sympathy can be seen on their faces when they confirm the cold fact that Petri told me earlier, that unfortunately our child has been dead for several hours. The heart curve would just be a flat line. Nothing can be done. They are focused on saving me.

- How is this possible? Everything was fine in the morning. I try to say, but no one hears, or at least can't answer, as they focus on saving me.

- 1.3 liters of blood have already been lost. Threat to life. She needs to be rushed to the hospital right now.

I hear isolated sentences from somewhere in the distance as I am being lifted onto a stretcher.

- We don't know how this is going go, she has lost and is still losing a lot of blood. The nurses tell a shocked Petri as they leave.

My memories are precarious flashes. The children woke up to my screams. Everything is a fog in my head. I am quickly transferred to an ambulance. Petri has to prepare for the worst. The bleeding becomes pulpy again. My father sits quietly in the front seat of the ambulance. The whistles sound and the ambulance accelerates to full speed. I can feel the speedbumps on the road, but I don't care. My baby is dead. The person supervising me talks to another Hospital and states that the situation is extremely serious, because they must drive all the way to Hospital in Helsinki. My blood pressure is 75/44 and I am still gushing out blood. I hear the nurse's heated conversation on the radio, where she emphasizes that the caesarean section being prepared in the operating room must be stopped or the patient arriving in their car will die.

My father sits in the front seat, completely silent. I have only seen my father cry once when his own mother became seriously ill. Now he is so terrified that he cannot even cry, scream or speak. He just concentrates on holding on as the ambulance flies by. The pace assures him that I'm still alive, there's still hope. If only the pace didn't slow down. My father is at a loss, there is nothing he can do to help me. He and my mother have always done anything for us, always found a way to help. When I was in a serious bike accident when I was young and I was lying on the edge of a ditch, while paramedics were supporting my torn hamstring and twisted neck, my father came to the scene of the accident calling my name. He wanted to help the ambulance crew. There is nothing he can do now. All I can do is try to stay alive. The blue light of ambulance whistles breaks the spring night sky like lightning. When the whistles are blowing, I can no longer even hear the comforting words of the paramedic. The time to deal with grief would be later. My father sits completely still.

At home, Melissa watches sadly as Petri cleans the pool of blood on his knees, while crying hysterically. Petri has lost his child. He doesn't know if he will also lose his life partner tonight. Will he wake up the next morning as a single parent, even though the night before the whole family celebrated the new addition to the family? Cleaning up the blood with a small hand towel is hopeless, but at least he can try to do something in a situation where there is nothing to be done. My mother strokes Petri's back and tries to comfort him, even though she herself is afraid of losing me and mourns the baby.

The ambulance stops in the hospital yard, and they lift me inside. I am examined and treated quickly. Slowly, the tiredness starts to take over and as I fall asleep, I make a silent wish that all this was just a bad dream.

I wake up early in the morning to the light coming from the slits in the hospital window blinds. I guess all the night's events were true. The wave of the hand I saw in the ultrasound the day before was not a greeting of seeing you soon, but a goodbye. The worried nurse brings me the phone: - Say something into the phone. There is your child who has cried all night and was afraid of losing you. I whisper into the phone: - Mother is here.

Our child cries and screams: - Mother! Mum!

Petri says that Melissa was afraid that she would lose her other mother as well. Her biological mother had died when the child was very young. It feels terrible what the children, Petri and my parents had to experience at night. The saddest thing is that Matias didn't get the chance to live. Even in this situation, I find myself thinking of others, even though I myself have been close to the gates of death.

I didn't have a chance to say goodbye to the baby at night. The nurse brings papers that should be filled out for burial. I'm talking to the priest about how I can ever get through this. Of course, for the sake of the children, I can wake up and continue, but will I ever really move on? Can you survive the loss of a child? How does it affect my everyday life, am I constantly afraid for the children? Even if no solution is found, the conversation with the priest is a positive experience. I'm glad he doesn't say everything has a purpose, fortunately. There can be no purpose to this. None of my children should have to be buried. I just have one question: why? The priest doesn't have an answer for that, but he has a lot of comforting words to give. They are enough for that moment. For a moment I can move forward again.

That night I became the mother of a small baby, but too small to live in the world with us. At night I became the mother of an angel child. Petri says that he called my supervisor. He couldn't get a single sensible word out of his mouth because of his crying, but the message had reached my supervisor. He had listened and comforted Petri. Fortunately, there was yet another warm-hearted supervisor and an understanding, good employer.

Petri has also been in contact with kindergarten and schoolteachers. The children are out of school. Children have no strength left for sadness. They deal with the grief of loss in different ways. One pours out his heart to friends, the other clears his head alone in the whirlwind of movies and the internet. The third tells everyone exactly what happened again and again. And describes it as precisely as if they were describing a crime thriller that they was watching from the outside, even though they had been a part of it.

The next evening, I get home from the hospital. After Matias, I don't want our own children to experience anything bad again. Life must go on. I sit on the edge of the bed with tears in my eyes. The floor looks cloudy. There's no rush for anything now. The empty lap is unexpectedly filled with a pile of white fur. A wet muzzle pokes my chin as if to ask how I am. My dear dog. Grateful and happy, it leans against me, although my gratitude towards the dog is much greater. A furry friend saved me mentally again. I pet the dog and lift my friend to the foot of the bed. I'm falling asleep. Nightmares wake me up again at night. When I wake up, I'm lonely. The dog is alert to help when I do, I don't want to wake up others for support. In happy dreams, I get to be with those I have already lost for a while. Waking up feels bad, even though I'm grateful at the same time.

Forward

Luckily, it's the weekend. Our children are highly independent. I wondered if it was natural or if they just had to learn to survive in these waves that life has given to us. We need to get ourselves oriented and consider how life will continue. We decide to cook something delightful with the children and watch a movie in the evening. We want to book a camper van for the summer. Yes, things will still work out somehow.

I rest on the couch and stare at the ceiling. I am thinking that the old bulbs should be replaced with brighter ones, although the light does not solve my real problem. Sinking into the dark void creates such a physical phenomenon. I got something else to think about, even for a moment. I don't have the energy left in me to change the bulbs. I will continue my life in obscurity for a while, I need to rest and recover because my body is broken. I force myself to work as soon as my physical condition allows it. I can't stop yet.

We will bury Matias only with the children because I don't have the strength to organize a bigger funeral. Before Matias is cremated, we take a picture of the children and our dog with a cute towel in which we wrap Matias. Saying goodbye together is now important for our family. The children write messages and draw pictures in the box where Matias will be cremated. Our pictures and thoughts would end up in the urn.

In a conflicted state, I go to talk to the priest before blessing the urn and descending to the ground. We belong to a church, but my thoughts are confused. How can God allow this to happen to such an innocent baby and to us? Fortunately, the priest is gentle, and I find the moment of conversation very therapeutic.

When we bury Matias, I also bury in my heart all our little ones who died in early pregnancy. The time after Matias's death was very dark for us parents for a long time. The children's everyday life continues, but it is difficult for us to go out. Babies passing by on the street remind us of our painful loss. Many who have experienced a miscarriage soon get pregnant again naturally and have a baby, but for us it is impossible. I don't know how to get out of the pit of despair and how bottomless sadness could turn into beautiful longing.

The children had really hoped for a baby and wondered if the matter could be resolved somehow. We have always wanted to answer their questions honestly, taking age into account. The children have asked, for example, if they could fix my stomach. It has always been easy and natural for children to talk about Matias, even though Matias was dead. From time to time they have wondered how old Matias would be at any given time.

After the burial, I experience a couple of confusing situations. One day, while visiting the grave again, a big fluffy bumblebee lands on my hand. I freak out but it doesn't do anything. That's all there is to it. When I leave the grave, the furry remains on the tombstone. Another miracle of nature takes place in our backyard on the terrace. As I sit there, a baby squirrel suddenly jumps into my lap. We take photos of it with the children and suddenly the baby squirrel jumps on the doll's pram in the yard. The children decide that the squirrel's name will be Lucky Squirrel. Matias' second name on the tombstone is Onni, meaning luck or happiness. Nature is a wonderful comforter. I often walk alone on beach on Espoo. There is something very comforting about the sea and the view.

At Christmas, we visit Matias's grave with the children. We parents have tears in our eyes. Matias is not with us to receive Santa Claus.

We light the candles and are silent. Gugu takes over the situation with the immediacy and calmness of a child. He bends down and, tilting his head to the ground, exclaims in a voice that can be heard on the ground: - Ho Ho Ho, Merry Christmas to you Matias down there!

Everyone smiles at Gugu's cheery reaction.

- Merry Christmas, dear Matias. I say and we go home. My angel child is with me in my dreams. Despite the sadness, it's Christmas and a new, hopefully better year will start soon.

You'll stay in my dreams when you're an angel now
May the others on the road to heaven protect you

There is no one to be seen, and in my rooms, only now is the wind blowing
We are once, and only that much
As we are given time [13]

New beginning. I realise that in order to survive, we have to pack up the past and find happiness and gratitude for what we have together now. We need to have time to stop and celebrate the five of us who survived. I suggest to Petri that we go to Spain and renew our wedding vows. He is surprised. He would probably be able to continue anyway, but it's important to me, so we book the trip. I want to do it in Spain. I have a lot of good memories from there since my own childhood. Children run there on the beach like me and my sister when we were little. However, I can't relax, because there are too many risks in the sea. The sea current could take away even a skilled swimmer. Petri swam in the deep end and I'm closer to beach with the children between us. We are like hawks watching over their young. I don't know how old the children have to grow before I am able to give more freedom.

After everything we've been through, we're celebrating fifteen years of marriage and the fact that we're still going together in the same direction. We chose the beautiful rock-cut chapel of Mijas on Costa del son in southern Spain as the place. We have been to Fuengirola with the children before. We meet the priest of the local Finnish parish and tell our story. It is important that the children are involved. Our journey is a kind of survival rite for all of us, and a end and a new beginning.

We have Casual white clothes. With us in the chapel there are people praying and tourists admiring the beauty of the place. When the priest enters the altar, people become quiet, some sneak away, but many stay in the back rows to see what is happening. The priest blesses our union and our family. She pays attention to the children and talks to them nicely. The place becomes important to all of us. We take pictures to remember, for which the amazing landscape draws a beautiful background. Children are excitedly waiting for ice cream and the restaurant located in the square. Everything is beautiful and happy. In my heart, however, I feel an aching, distant sadness. As we walk towards the ice cream parlour, I look at Petri and the children and think in my mind that our family is not complete yet and I am not whole.

You can smile for the camera
And still be sad inside
Everyone is looking for ways to stay sane
Everything should be perfect
A pure white dream from a magazine
What life cannot disturb
I don't want pure hell
I prefer laughter and dust
To be whole when broken [14]

On the walls of infertility clinics and hospital waiting rooms, I have noticed invitations to peer support groups for those who have experienced a miscarriage and lost their baby. I don't know how they could help me or us, when there isn't enough time between work and treatments to even take care of myself or the relationship. The children's everyday life has had to continue, and their happiness has come before my own well-being.

Many people who have passed by our house may have wondered why our piles of leaves remain under the snow or why the bicycles are not put in storage when winter comes. Someone has said that we are relaxed when it is not always completely cool. It would be great if you could fix everything. However, in the midst of infertility treatments, hormone storms, contract texts, adoption reports and all the sorting out and running the children's everyday life, there is absolutely no time to put up and decorate a beautiful home. We fix things a little at a time within the framework of the children, the adoption of children, the time allowed by work and our ability to cope. We need to prioritize in everything. Our life, with rest breaks, is a game of minutes until the four children are home.

Of course, I try to be relaxed amid all the chaos. Constantly trying makes everyday life too stiff. It's just hard to slow down and believe that by doing less, I could give more to my children and loved ones. We keep the basics in order, but otherwise we might cut the corners a bit. Good enough is good enough for us. Children has clean socks to wear at school, but they won't die if the socks are a different pair.

However, I'm not ready to stop until the last option has been tried. One of my wise managers once said at work that the dogs are barking but the caravan is moving. The goal and direction should be kept clear in mind. I decide not to give up, even if the path ahead is completely covered in fog.

Metalbed

The infertility clinic calls and asks how to deal with the couple of embryos we have. I look horrified when I catch my empty gaze in the mirror. In order to survive, I had completely closed this fact out of my mind. We still have embryos left. I can't experience it all again right away. I don't want to give my children any more useless wishes and sadness. I reply that I will call back soon. We chat with Petri and conclude that we can't wait either. We have to find a way go through this in secret again and mentally externalize ourselves from the matter. I call the clinic and say that we can get started right away. I feel physically recovered from the miscarriage after all.

At this point, neither of us can believe in success anymore, but we can't stop either, because no one has found any reason for the miscarriages. Matias's pregnancy went well at the beginning, and the fertility clinic encourages us to try again. There's nothing to suggest that the next time can't be successful. A massive miscarriage last time doesn't mean it will happen this time. We don't want to tell anyone about this.

The first embryo dies before the transfer and the last one is revived. The clinic states that it could be transferred. I am silent while they transfer the embryo. I just made sure that I took the medicine and follow the instructions during pregnancy. Otherwise, I lock the matter in the recesses of my mind and deny myself the opportunity to think about it. We watch funny programs with the children and Petri, and everyday life goes on as if there was no pregnancy.

Weeks pass as I go to my necessary doctor's appointments without any enthusiasm. The doctors must be amazed at my insensitivity. I am not in contact with the nurse office at all either. I am surprised when I realize that the structural ultrasound is approaching fast. The almost non-existent optimism is slowly starting to rear its head. There is still something strange about this pregnancy. My feelings are different than they were when I was carrying Topias or Matias. Worried, I go to the clinic, where an ultrasound examination confirms my suspicions: the growth of the fetus has slowed down and the development no longer corresponds to the weeks of pregnancy. The child would not grow up to be a viable person. The pregnancy must be terminated, and I would give birth to a dead child.

I'm at the Women's Clinic again. For the first time, I am waiting for the termination of the pregnancy, the death of the child and the birth of my dead child. I didn't think I could experience anything more terrible. I need to push my dead child out of me. In the past, everything has happened unexpectedly. Now I must live a painful night knowing that I will have to give birth, which will end in pain and inconsolable sadness.

I cannot sleep. The nurses bring a metal bucket with a seat on the edge to my bed. I'm shocked to give birth to it. That metal bucket would be my child's death bed. Never! However, that's the way it has to be. After hours of pain, my dead child comes out and we help him with a soft landing in the corner of the bucket. He is like a withered flower on a metal bed. The little one has tried everything but is exhausted in the whirlwind of the surrounding circumstances and my broken womb. There is no end to my crying, not yet.

We decide to mourn our loss together this time. It would be too heavy to put our loved ones once again through the emotional storm that Matias's death and my own situation caused to everyone. The hospital stay is not long, so we don't have to explain anything to anyone. They were women's problems.

Before we have time to think about how we would progress with our dream of four children next, the new Women's Clinic is interested in my medical history. The doctors decide to find out thoroughly this time what causes my series of miscarriages. I am going through many studies and am waiting for answers. Maybe there would finally be a solution or even an explanation for my situation.

After the examinations, the doctor states that the child's death was caused by the cessation of the functioning of the placenta and the abnormality of the front wall of my uterus. I can't have children and my successful pregnancy with Topias has been lucky. The doctor's words are first followed by emptiness. At the same time, it's the end point that the pregnancies are over for me. It is easier to know what causes miscarriages. Now I know that for medical reasons, trying again is pointless. I feel angry that this was not noticed earlier, even though doctors have been aware of the effects of the symptoms for years. We are unsure if we will ever realize our dream of a family of four children.

I V

The Secret decision

I find myself regressing and getting stuck in the past. Seeing other mothers and their babies causes pain again and in the company of babies I turn my eyes away from them. I need to cope for the sake of my children, motherhood and life. I carry out everyday life routinely.

In the middle of our happiness the Topias's babyhood was also difficult due to reflux. Plus, everything was new and uncertain. In adoptions, we also had happy moments with our children, even though family life started with a toddler or small child. We have lived with a strong longing for a baby and baby time that comes with it. Baby would be the fourth leaf in the clover. Parenting with a small child has also partly been quite sort of the financial constraints arising from the treatments, we have not been able to afford to stay at home for a long time. If only we could still have the baby and stay home with them.

Matias left our children with a strong longing for a baby. They had already had time to get excited about their little brother. My sister, who lives in the house next door, has a baby in the midst of my grief, which brings a lot of joy and relief to our children in the midst of our grief.

As our longing for a baby continues, I'm starting to desperately look for any option. Would there be another possibility? Surrogacy. I know that surrogacy has not been possible in Finland for a couple of years. Giving infertility treatments leading to adoption was prohibited by law. In Finland, the surrogate is the child's legal mother, and the transfer of parentage requires adoption. When I get to know the matter in more detail, it becomes clear that surrogacy abroad would be possible. There are a lot of involuntarily childless people, and the decision-makers hope that more children would be brought to Finland. There is declining birth rate in Finland and there is ongoing discussion on how to improve it. So why are the infertility treatments needed for surrogacy not allowed in Finland, and to get them you have to travel abroad? This often excludes those who want to become parents and who cannot financially afford to go abroad. The potential social problems prevented by the ban on surrogacy are, I believe, better manageable in Finland than in some of the countries to which the current legislation directs desperate couples like us. If more children are wanted in Finland, then society would have to support those who want to become parents in different ways. Fortunately, we both have jobs, so foreign Surrogacy is financially possible for us.

In Finland's child strategy, the goverment wants to promote the birth rate and increase work-based immigration. The problem with this thinking is that not everyone can get pregnant normally. There should be more support and opportunities for that. Increasing family leave or increasing family allowances will not help those who want to increase the birth rate but do not have the possibility of getting pregnant. Part of the state subsidies should be directed towards enabling fertility treatments with open eyes. International adoption rarely offers the opportunity to experience baby time with a child, which many parents hope to experience.

In public and in social media discussions, some people blame those who started the surrogacy process. They are even talking about it as if you are ordering or buying a child. People don't always know how to put themselves in the position of unintentionally childless people. They may not have been in the same situation themselves, where it is easy to criticize and shout from the side-lines. We can't tell anyone about our plans when we don't know how other people feel. We don't want to add to our burden of possible negative comments from others in a difficult situation anyway. At worst, our entire process could be jeopardized if someone intervened in the wrong way. Families are different. Why shouldn't we pursue our happiness that doesn't take away the happiness of others? It can't be wrong to be the master of yourself and your own happiness?

Did I remember to be my own master
Did I remember to do as I please
Did I remember to give thanks, show appreciation
Did I remember to take my time?
If this was my last night
Could I be happy
Did I remember to be my own master today too [15]

We are aware of our age, but we don't want to hear discouraging comments on this topic either. We are already in our forties, but we haven't chosen to be at this stage of having children until now, and even if we had chosen, wouldn't it be our own decision? The most important thing is that the future child, in addition to us, has a lot of safety net around him, should something happen. We become parents at many ages. A happy example of this is our current president, who became a father at an older age after long wishing for a child with his wife. Fortunately, responsible work and parenting a small child can be combined in Finland, as long as you have a child first.

It's hard to start a process that has to be done in secret from everyone. There is no one to talk to or give advice. We have no information about surrogacy. We need to try to figure everything out ourselves. There is also no information about subsidies from the National social support institute. There is no model for surrogacy and no one answers our questions. It will be sorted out along the way if or when we have a baby. I guess we just have to take the financial and mental risk.

We have no other choice but to gather courage again and head abroad. We are starting to find out the options offered by different countries. We hear about a good clinic in St. Petersburg, where the director is a doctor who studied in Finland. We are in contact there. The clinic's employees provide friendly guidance and tell that two different organizations are involved in the process. In one, infertility treatments are handled, and in the other, surrogacy, pregnancy monitoring and the birth itself. We receive a large number of documents, legal and contractual texts, as well as information about the process and its costs in English. When the children go to bed at night, we go through the papers, list new questions and write messages to the clinic. There is still no one to ask in Finland. I hear from a journalist about a couple who had two children from St. Petersburg and everything went well. We agreed on an anonymous call. During that phone call, our decision is confirmed: we are going to St. Petersburg.

I am in telephone contact with clinics and at the same time I am learning a lot about legal and contractual matters. Petri is growing into his role as the father of a small baby who is leaving for St. Petersburg. We are about to embark on an exciting and partly unplanned trip. In addition to cooperation and division of workload, we must dare to reflect on ourselves and one's own feelings and to tell the other about them. The differences and strengths of Petri's and mine's characters will be particularly highlighted in this project. Petri is excited to leave for the unknown without a safety net, like he used to when leaving for Kenya. Now we would leave in secret without telling anyone. Petri is sceptical about the success of our plan because something surprising always happens to us. In addition, surrogacy is expensive and complicated. This is not a problem for me, because I believe that things will work out as long as we don't give up. Like they say, the one who asks will find the way. Petri would like everything to be fully clarified in advance. As a counterweight to uncertainty, Petri's absolute strength is paper warfare. Even in a hurry, he quickly assimilates a legal text in a foreign language and finds the points that need clarification.

One of my biggest fears is if the woman working as a surrogate would want to keep the baby. The clinic assures us that the contracts are legally binding in Russia and they will help us find legal help if, despite everything, my fears come true. The donor only signs the final documents regarding the relinquishment of the child after the child is born, so we cannot get complete guarantee on the matter in advance.

Soon we are in a situation where we both realize that we cannot prepare things further than this. We just have to move forward again. The paperwork and legal matters have been sorted out as best as we can. We can't ask for help from anyone. According to Russian law, we would be the parents of the child to be born, but according to Finnish law, the woman who gave birth is the mother. Based on the court decisions that Petri read online, the father's position may also have to be discussed in court for a long time. This creates tension, but we will not give up. Like so many times before, nothing would be as certain as uncertainty.

Golden ring

For us to go on short trips in St. Petersburg, for the sake of our children's care, we need to tell my parents about it. My own parents are the biggest support. They don't question our decision or criticize, instead they are always present, listen and want to understand things that are new to them from our point of view too. After all, it's about our lives. We don't tell the children because a possible new loss would be too painful for them after Matias. We can't talk about it with others either. The whole process is still so full of question marks that we don't want to discuss the topic. Since Topias was a child, we have taken small breaks regularly, so our trips do not arouse suspicion in our close circle or in our children.

Our first trip to St. Petersburg is coming soon. We go to the clinic and start preparing for surrogacy as well. St. Petersburg can be reached from Finland by ship, plane and train. In the next two years, we would become familiar with all the options.

St. Petersburg is a beautiful and international city, located 300 kilometres from Helsinki. St. Petersburg is a big city with a population greater than the whole of Finland. For some reason, this number of people is not visible in the street view, but the city feels spacious, even though there are people everywhere. St. Petersburg is the second largest city in Russia and the world's northernmost city with a million inhabitants. As its name suggests, the city was founded by Emperor Peter the Great as his administrative seat in 1703. The city is located at the bottom of the Gulf of Finland in the estuary of the Neva River, a little further south than Helsinki. Helsinki has the northernmost metro line in the world. Also in St. Petersburg, the backbone of public transport is a functional subway system. The center of St. Petersburg has wonderful architecture and it's easy to get around. The Neva River divides the city in several canals, where canal cruises are organized in the summer, like Venice or Amsterdam. For a lover of art and culture, St. Petersburg is surprisingly close to Finland. Petri remembers his first visit as a child to St. Petersburg, or Leningrad, as the city was named at the time. Petri remembers the city boulevards wider than the Finnish highways, where only a few cars drove. Today, things are different. The city centre is really congested and full of more expensive Western luxury cars.

It's soothing to walk in St. Petersburg's parks and dream that one day we'd be pushing our little ones in strollers here. We go to souvenir shops and buy a small dog soft toy for the future baby. We are clearly beginning to trust cautiously that our children's little sister or little brother would still be real one day. What else could go wrong?

We get a lot of help from the clinics. Since English is not spoken nearly everywhere, Google translate is useful.

When choosing a surrogate, it is important to us that she already has her own child. Although the contracts are comprehensive and we feel safe, it seems that it would be easier for the donor to give up the child when she is already a mother. She should be healthy and motivated to want to help the childless. It would also be good if she had done this before with some other couple earlier. In this way, the surrogate is known to keep the contract.

The first woman found for surrogacy meets all our other criteria but has not had a surrogacy before. The pregnancies start and progress well, but she has two miscarriages. We are already running out of embryos and we can no longer risk it. As despair starts to creep in, we get a call from the clinic. They would have a nice woman there as a surrogate who had just successfully delivered a baby for another couple and would be willing to help us as well. This is reassuring news. We decide to go ahead with her. We get comprehensive information about her, and the decision is easy. The embryo is transferred and then the painful waiting, familiar to us through my own pregnancies, begins. Fortunately, the embryo is not inside me this time and the baby would have at least some hopes of surviving.

In a couple of weeks, we will receive happy news. The pregnancy has started successfully, and the hormone level is high. Everything seems to be progressing smoothly. We constantly receive information about the progress of the pregnancy, the health of the surrogate, the results of blood tests and other necessary information. Everything we wish for is answered. The baby is given a NIPT test and based on that she is a healthy girl. If all goes well, she will be our dear little girl. We have decided she will be named Tessa, again based on the names of our other children's names. It's really wonderful to get this type of news. However, a familiar fear, a dark figure looms in the background with all our past losses. I'm afraid to look at the ultrasound images and video sent by the clinic. I just glance at them quickly, because I can't get attached, at least not yet. Matias' waving in my womb is still too fresh in my memory. The day will soon come when we will get a 4D image and see the baby's face. It feels as if the heart stops in place for a moment, it is such a comprehensively exciting sight. The sweet little mouth and her smile are now so close and at the same time further away than ever – in a foreign land, in the womb of a foreign mother.

It's the third trimester of pregnancy and the cold wind is starting to blow again. The cervix has started to shorten for some reason. The dark figure wraps her cloak around me again. I'm afraid of miscarriage and I feel suffocating. The baby must be taken out safely, even it means she is here early. The clinic says that there is a golden ring for these situations. The ring is put on to protect the pregnancy in order to make it continue as long as possible. At this point, I wondered why I haven't heard of this in Finland. Could it have helped me? Maybe it wouldn't be because my placenta didn't work. We try to live a normal life amidst our secret. During Topias's pregnancy, everyone was tense with us. Now nobody knows what we are going through. I try to maintain a shell around me and focus on work. Every moment of waiting becomes agonizing again. Every time the phone rings, I'm sure it's sad news from the clinic.

However, the pregnancy progresses well with the help of the ring. The surrogate mother conscientiously takes it easy and rests a lot. According to the contract, she will follow the doctors' instructions. After the summer, we are already in safe weeks. The baby is doing very well. The doctors estimated that the baby would still be born prematurely. There would be enough excitement until the end, but mainly only with legal matters, unlike in my births.

We tell our supervisors at work about the situation, and they are genuily happy for us, especially since they know our background and previous losses. We say we are going to pick up the child. We don't want to tell anyone about surrogacy. At this point, it's "adoption", which it really is. According to Finnish law, I have to eventually adopt a child in Finland through intra-family adoption. Although according to Russian law I am directly the mother of the baby, according to Finnish law the woman who gave birth is the mother. From Finland's point of view, the child has only one parent, and that is father, Petri. I tell my supervisor that there are uncertainties in the matter. We decide to follow the progress of the situation for a while before we tell more about it at my workplace. The time for the substitute arrangement would be a little later.

In the eye of the Storm

I watch the news about the events in Russia with concern. Putin has been elected president again and there are riots and disorder in several cities. I hope everything is fine politically when we go on the maternity trip. No reason should stop our journey. When we visited the infertility clinic in St. Petersburg, everything was always good and calm. Even strangers are friendly and helpful in the city. We see only one police situation during our travels, when someone was forcibly arrested at the corner of the Winter palace square.

During the winter and spring, I have started to have severe headaches, which are often diagnosed as migraines in occupational health care. Even a neurologist agrees. Muscle pain in the muscles of the head is also offered as the reason. The pain feels strange and always in the same place. It is difficult to travel, especially abroad for intensive training, when the pain makes it difficult to concentrate and cope. I feel weak, even though the trainings are usually held in nearby countries and the flights are short.

The heavy grind of work is interrupted by the happy news that the next business trip would be to Hawaii, and I could take Petri with me. We get to stay there for a long weekend alone after the program organized for the employees is over. In addition to the official program, we have time for romantic dinners, walks on the dark seashore, driving on jungle roads and snorkelling with sea turtles. The journey feels like a new beginning. The life-threatening miscarriage is over. I had finally received an explanation and a point for more than a decade of infertility treatments. The baby we've been waiting for a long time is being carried by the surrogate and at least it's still safe. Nothing would come in the way of our happiness anymore.

The storm begins. In September 2019, everything in my life will change, as it did after receiving a letter about infertility, which I consider the beginning of the second phase of my life. Now the third phase of my life begins.

I'm sitting in the office at the desk across from my colleague. The work doesn't really seem to be progressing, because for some reason typos keep appearing on the screen. I wonder out loud what's wrong with this keyboard? Completely different letters appear on the screen than what I type. My colleague helpfully stands up and walks next to me to clarify the situation. He asks to press the letter T. I press the key, but a completely different letter appears on the screen. He says I didn't press T and tells me to try again. I will try again without success. He thinks I'm somehow strained or some muscle is stuck. I decide to go to the sofa and lay down for a while. He helps me up. When I get up, I notice that my legs don't work normally, and my vision starts to deteriorate. We decide to go to a nearby medical center.

Even on the stairs at work, the right side of my field of vision starts to blur completely. It feels like there is a storm in the eye. I think I'm going to have a seizure. My co-worker helps me sit up to call an ambulance. More staff from my workplace run to help and help me lie down on the couch. A large black and white serrated strip suddenly begins to cross my field of vision. I now feel like I'm having a seizure and I tell my colleague to take Petri's number from me quickly before I lose consciousness. I groan and start listing the number. My colleague calls Petri. The ambulance comes quickly, and they interpret my situation as a migraine attack, which I have been diagnosed with before. I am transported to near-by Haartman Hospital, where I get a "migraine cocktail" for my headache. I fall asleep on medication. When I wake up, the seizure is gone and I get to go home. Everything points to a severe migraine attack.

The next day, the pains continue to be severe. Mole fever had temporarily taken my sight years before and it shouldn't happen again, so it's not mole fever. I haven't had any flu, so it couldn't have been an after-disease either. My alert supervisor sends me to occupational health. He says I need a head scan, by any means necessary. A doctor experienced in occupational health rules out migraine. Migraine does not affect the motor skills of the hands; this is about something more serious. He writes me a referral for further tests at the hospital. At the hospital, the nurse does not agree with the need for imaging. Dozens of people complaining of headaches come to the hospital every day, they can't scan them all. I tell my whole story and she fetches a doctor. The young male doctor decides that a photograph of the head is still necessary just to be sure. I don't remember anything about the description. After the photoshoot, I'm in the changing room putting on clothes when the nurse who did the photoshoot comes to me and says the scariest words of my life: - Don't leave yet, the doctor looked at the pictures and you have some black area in your head.

Petri is finishing the last tasks of the working day. When I call him, I ask Petri to come to Hospital right away, because they found something in my head. I send a message to my other loved ones, my supervisor and my co-worker. I am transferred to the neurology ward. I sit in the corridor and stare in front of me as if in a dream. Petri would arrive at the hospital quickly and my parents soon after. Will this not only be a fight for my baby's survival, but also a fight for my survival? I'm more scared than ever. When I was fighting for my life in the ambulance after the miscarriage, I hadn't even had time to be afraid of my sadness. Now there is time to think, but I am not alone with my thoughts. The dark figure laughs with a screeching voice that drowns out the sounds of the arriving ambulances.

I'm waiting on my bed. An empathic nurse comes to me. He is experienced and friendly. He says that the lump on my head looks sharp. In his experience, that's a good thing. So, there is some hope. I caught the end of the rope again, which had slipped from my hands in the waves. Fortunately, this friendly nurse threw a rope. He had the courage to say something, because most nurses wouldn't, since according to rules that only doctors are allowed to comment results of any medical examination. For this moment, a little hope is important.

The nurse reminds me of the man I spoke to on the emergency phone when I found out about our infertility. At that time, he told me about his neighbour's adoption, and it was in that moment a lifeline for me to keep going. The words prevented the impending collapse.

My head will be scanned more closely, but I need to wait in the hospital for the results overnight until the following afternoon. How can I sleep while waiting for the result? My parents and Petri are with me in the hospital in the evening, but in the end Petri has to go home to the children and I will be alone. I sit in the corridor and watch a light casual TV series on my phone, so I could forget where I am. I sneak into the room only when I almost fall asleep in the hallway. I can only go to bed when I am completely tired and sure that I will fall asleep right away. I can't be awake alone in the dark, so I don't drown under the negative and scary thoughts. What will happen to our child in St. Petersburg if I have a tumour on my head that needs to be operated? How do we get her? Will there be any problems with intra-family adoption if I'm no longer healthy? How do we get through all this?

All the disasters you feared came true,
came the flood and came a thousand floods,
but you still swim.[16]

Disappeared father

Where is your husband? This is a question that my friends and neighbours are cautiously trying to ask. In the queue at the grocery store, I hear some people talking about us. They reflected on our difficulties, especially my life-threatening miscarriage. They wonder why Petri is not seen when everything should be fine now. I back up and quietly exit to the back left with my head down. I still need to hide the truth to protect everyone. I sit in my father's car. How did it end up like this? I get lost in my thoughts and relive the events in disbelief.

We are sitting in hospital with Petri. On the other side of the table, the surgeon explains in detail the progress and details of the upcoming operation. Petri listens attentively and asks clarifying questions. That's good, because I'm too exhausted myself to think about anything extra. I'm just focusing on getting through the surgery one day at a time. In the MRI scan (magnetic resonance imaging), I had received some reassuring information: the black area visible in the image was a tumour, but it is not located in the brain but on the meninges. According to the prognosis, the tumour is benign, but to be sure, it must be removed. My skull would be opened so that the true nature of the tumour could be confirmed with a pathological examination.

I wake up when the surgeon tells me that the tumour is stuck in the optic nerve. The risk of surgery is that I will be left with a black area in my field of vision, the size of which is unknown. I ask if I still have even a small strip of vision. The doctor answers that vision is usually preserved at least to some extent. It's enough for me. I wish would be able to see my children again after the operation.

The doctor notices my long hair. He warns that too many come to surgery with their hair shaved and tells me not to shave my hair. During the operation, the entire head is not opened, because the incision is only from the back of the head to the neck and the opening is to the left. Petri teases the idea with the surgeon and asks a few more questions. Sometimes I wonder how callously yet clinically Petri reacts to such a serious matter, but I understand that this is his way of coping. Creating an accurate understanding of the future measures and strong trust in the experts pushes worries to the back burner. Petri does not give power to fears like mine but tries to move the matter forward in a systematic way.

It's the day of the surgery. I sit on the edge of the bed. In front of me are four blank papers and a ballpoint pen. There is half an hour. I am wondering what I should write for our children.

"Now that you're reading this, from the surgery I've gone to the angels.
You are okey, dad and everyone else are there for you, you'll be fine.
You are a lively and such a amazing person!
You will still have a wonderful life.
Always remember that I love you.
Everything will be all right.
Focus on the good things in your life and think positively.
with love,
Mum".

I can't see anything from my crying when I finish the letters to my three oldest children.

The nurse will announce that it's my turn. Help, what should I write in a hurry to the youngest who is still in the surrogate mother's womb? I decide that Petri will be able to tell her in time how much I wanted her. I swallow my cry. The nurse signals to leave.

I'm alive! When I open my eyes, all I see is fog. Everything is very bright. There is a figure on the left, but I can't turn to look at it because of my pain. For some reason my arm hurts more than my head.

- Your vision is still bad when the tumour was around the optic nerve. Your vision will improve little by little, don't worry. A friendly voice reassures and continues: - You are in the intensive care unit. I'm your nurse, call if you need anything.

He moves to the other side of me to sit on the computer. He's very close. It feels safe. Even a whisper would be enough to get help if no sound comes out of my mouth. Someone is shouting behind me. I don't dare say anything about my arm pain. I'm alive. I want the grieving man to get all the attention and help he needs now. He must need help. The situation was another in a bicycle crash I experienced when I was young, where a racing cyclist drove towards me. He lay lifeless on the ground. I could not move either because of my thigh and neck injury. When the ambulances came, I shouted to help him first. After a while, the paramedics came to me and snorted that the man was fine. He is just upset about the broken bike so much that he refuses to get up. Now on the other hand the painful cry heard next to me, tells of real distress.

The man's pain is brought under control and the situation calms down. I whisper to talk to my doctor. I ask when he will come to me. The nurse replies that she will be coming soon. I have something important to tell for him.

The doctor says the operation was successful as planned and the tumour has been sent for analysis. Radiation treatments are needed, but the amount needed will only be known more precisely when the quality of the tumour is known. I want to whisper something to the doctor. He bends over with confusion and turns his head to hear my point. Amid my sobs, I silently say that I can't die, my beloved baby is in another person's womb in St. Petersburg. I ask the doctor not to tell anyone, that no one will make it difficult for me to get to my child. The doctor thanks me for the trust and says that he will do everything he can to make sure I make to the birth in St. Petersburg. He says that he can organize the schedules of radiation treatments so that I can visit abroad when it is necessary for the child's documents. I am forever grateful to the doctor.

When I finally get out of the intensive care unit, Petri and the children come to the hospital to see me. At first they are shocked and the room falls silent. Petri tells the children that everything is fine now and that the mother will recover. I lie on the bed on my stomach. Instead of a fairy tale princess, the children say that I would easily win first prize in the Halloween costume contest. The back of my head is covered in metal rivets from top to bottom. I try to see the children through my swollen eyes. I also look at Petri's relief expression after surviving the operation. I think he must really love me; a sense of duty alone wouldn't have brought us this far together.

I turn with difficulty towards the children and Petri. A strange scene of light floods my eyes. It feels like I'm in an amusement park machine, where different coloured lights, patterns and clowns are thrown into my eyes. I don't dare say anything to the children, so they don't get scared. The scene lasts only a few seconds. After that, I see the children as blurry figures, only a thin strip of clear vision to the left is present.

At night, the attacks become more frequent and violent. Fortunately, there is a medicine that helps them. Would there always be such bouncing light scenes in my life? Would the seizures become more frequent? Fortunately, there is a lane on the left side of my field of vision where I could still see my children, each of them. I am waiting to see even the smallest one that is yet to be born.

When the forces of a strange land
It would take you with it
No matter where I am
I will come back
I am by your side
May the beasts of the night be gone
Because I won't let it break you [17]

Often in a difficult moment, I listen to this song and let the tears come out. Famous Finnish pop singer, Mariska descriptively stated in the "Vain Elämää"- television show (based on the format "De beste zangers van Nederland") that tears are an brightener for the eyes[18]. I look at myself in the mirror and I think I look like a turkey. That I probably won't turn into a swan, but maybe at least a mallard. The song gives me strength to continue.

We meet a female doctor at the cancer clinic. I'm scared and waiting for the result of the tumour's quality. Fortunately, pathological examinations have confirmed that it is not a malignant tumour. However, the type of tumour is such that the number of radiation treatments increases from four to thirty. Radiation treatments have been postponed as much as it is safe, because first I would have to make it to St. Petersburg with Petri. As soon as the sight starts to return, we start preparing the trip to St. Petersburg so that we can get there before the birth. Before leaving, a mould will be made on my face, which would be used to attach me to the radiotherapy table. Mould casting is unpleasant. At the same time, I feel deep gratitude towards the Finnish healthcare system. Fortunately, I am getting the help that everyone in the world should be entitled to. After the mould is finished, I will be put on the radiotherapy table for the first time. My head is screwed to the table. I can't move at all to get the beams to hit the right spot. It's necessary, but when I'm strapped with a mask on my face, I feel like Anthony Hopkins' Hannibal Lecter in the movie

The Silence of the lambs. Tears come to my eyes when I think that I cannot die on this table without seeing my child even once.

Our departure to St. Petersburg is approaching. I've asked the children afterwards about the time in St. Petersburg. How did they feel when they didn't know where we really went on vacation and to get our memorable Christmas present? They just said that they thought for a long time about what kind of surprise we were going to get for them. What could be the best Christmas present ever? The wildest guesses had been a real pony or a sports car. On the phone they always asked where we were, and we said they would find out soon. Hopefully.

We travel to St. Petersburg on the Allegro which is a direct train connection between Helsinki and St. Petersbur, because I don't dare to get on a plane with my operated head yet. We will transfer the requested amount of money in cash to cover the expenses that arise from the surrogacy. We must declare the amount we are transporting at the border. For some reason, the Russian border authorities do not accept our form. Petri tries to follow the instructions and reads the long instructions from the papers while the clerk waits. This is where Petri and I differ. In acute situations, I don't take the time to read the instructions, instead I hand the pen to the clerk and, as I don't know the language, I ask him to show me how to fill out the form using sign language. He then shows that, in addition to the number, the sum must also be written on the line with letters. That's what I do and it's fine.

We stay in St. Petersburg in a chain hotel owned by a Finnish co-operative company. We are waiting every day for news about the baby's birth. The hotel staff is friendly, and we tell them why we are staying there for so long. Every ringing of the phone makes me wonder if it's time to leave. We take care of the necessary agency matters together with the clinic's lawyer. We visit agencies and sign documents with the interpreter. We walk around the hotel, admiring the scenery as much as I can after the surgery.

We are preparing for the birth of the baby by buying clothes and baby accessories from the city. St. Petersburg is also home to super-rich people who have their own shopping places. On one of our shopping trips, we enter one such department store from the street. We are ordinary Finnish tourists, quite neatly dressed, but we are not and do not look like millionaires. As soon as we enter the store, the security guard starts following us. I don't think this place is quite suitable for our payrate. Petri looks around and gently starts guiding me back towards the exit. I thought we have the right to visit the children's clothing section, we need a coverall and a hat for the baby. Heading to the escalator again. Petri notices the guard on the lower floor saying something into his earphones and the guard on the next floor turns to look in our direction. It's not a very pleasant shopping experience. I have still decided to buy something necessary for the baby. I notice the babies' clothes and carefully turn to reveal the price tag of the beautiful winter overalls. The overalls can remain in the store. The next shelf has pacifier cords in a basket. We need one and we can afford it, so I'll buy it. n the next store, we won't get guards after us. Since we don't have gold glitter on our heads, when we ask about the children's clothing department, the saleswoman immediately directs us to the discount clothing corner. We are laughing at our own casual appearance, but we hide it and politely go to look at discounted clothes. We found a good overall from a Finnish children's clothing brand. We buy it and head out.

The next step would be to find a breast milk formula. It is available in powder form in St. Petersburg's grocery store. We will buy it but we will try to find it also ready. It's not a simple thing when we try to find it by asking the locals for advice. They don't speak English. Following Google translator, we walk through pharmacies, shops and specialty stores, but nowhere is there liquid infant formula. We will make do with powder. Petri explains the instructions in Russian with the help of a picture translator. This is enough to feed our little girl during the trip. Everything begins to be concrete, and the girl is still alive. Now you just have to trust that everything will go well. Still, we are afraid of a lot.

My departure to Finland and the start of radiation treatments are fast approaching. Radiation cannot be moved without risking my health. Labor is still not started, and I have to return to Finland without seeing the baby. I sadly say goodbye to Petri and head towards the airport. I instruct the officers about my health situation. I give them a pre-written guide that tells them what I have and where they can call if something happens. The officers deliver the information to the captain and promise to monitor me more closely throughout the flight to Finland.

I was in St. Petersburg for two weeks waiting for the birth of our child. Heading home, I understand that we were called to the place in a hurry so that the paperwork would be ready when the child was born. Of course, there was always a risk that the labor would start prematurely. Petri's task now is to stay and wait alone.

Tears of happiness in distance

It is the beginning of November in 2019. I look in the mirror in the dressing room of the radiotherapy clinic. My thin hair frames my face. I don't want to touch the back of my head because I know it's bald. Instead of four radiation treatments, I was prescribed thirty radiation treatments. The quality of the tumour requires it to be completely removed. After the fifteenth radiation treatment, my hair starts to fall out. Fortunately, I don't have to think about that, because everyone at home, at work and elsewhere accepts me as I am. I'm grateful for that.

After the treatment, I get dressed. I feel the phone vibrate as I take my jacket off. I peek through the crack in the dressing room door, the nurse is still nowhere to be seen. I answer the call asking about Petri. The caller has been trying to reach Petri many times today and his phone is ringing. My throat tightens. Petri's whereabouts are being asked again. I'm trying to whip up something vague quickly. I state that it was left silent by accident. I'll tell that I'm just going to radiation therapy, I can't talk now, I'll get back to it. I can't tell anyone where Petri is. The secret is too big and the risks of someone messing up already otherwise uncertain plan are palpable. The situation is increasingly difficult. But Petri must announce that he is even alive. I send a message about the incoming call to him. Petri calls the questioner after a while and says that he is fine but does not say where he is. Not yet. Someone in the close circle already suspects that our marriage is falling apart after all the burden we've experienced, and that Petri just went off to think somewhere. Someone else thinks about how strange it is when the husband disappears at the same time as the wife is undergoing radiation treatments.

I'm sitting in my parents' living room with sunglasses on. Autumn has turned into winter and snowy ice covers the sea. The children go to school and my parents take turns taking care of me and the children at home. My light-spotted eyes still can't stand the light of day. On the way to St. Petersburg, I told about my surgery in the hotel so that wearing my sunglasses indoors and choosing a dark corner table in the restaurant would be better understood.

Everything is getting ready, and the labor would start soon. We decide to tell the kids. We explain that the father is picking up the little sister. If all goes well, we will soon have a little baby. The children are excited and wonder what Surrogacy means. I'll explain it by talking about my broken uterus. The children understand it easily and now we wait a little bit longer.

I've been in Finland for a couple of days when Petri calls and says he's in a taxi on his way to the maternity hospital. The childbirth has started! Now the suspense drama I've been waiting for begins. I can only wait with the phone in my hand. Petri goes to the hospital, which is less than an hour away from the centre of St. Petersburg. He arrives at the hospital with a backpack and stroller full of stuff, without his baby and wife. People wonder and look for another people belonging in his company. No one speaks English in the hospital lobby and the interpreter has not yet arrived. There are many large groups of relatives in the lobby with congratulatory flowers and balloons. Petri shows the security guard at the reception a Russian message written by our contact on his phone. It reads: "I am a father and I have come for my baby, who is being delivered by a surrogate and labor has begun." The security guard shakes his head in disbelief and doesn't understand at all what it is about. Petri calls the interpreter sent by the clinic. An interpreter is necessary, as no one in the hospital speaks English. After what seems like an endless wait, a stylized American English-speaking woman appears in the lobby. She has a short conversation in Russian with the guard. The doors open and Petri gets past the security guard to the hospital. The interpreter guides Petri to the third floor, where a barren, modestly furnished room awaits Petri and the baby. They would spend five nights in the hospital before being discharged home. Some of the hospital staff are amazed when they realize that the father comes to take care of the baby at the hospital alone and the mother is nowhere to be seen.

In the end, I get a picture on my phone of a little baby screaming while being weighed and another picture of her swaddled in a tight wrap. So cute! Finally, the baby is alive and here in the world. She's all right. I dare to be cautiously happy already. However, her smile is still unattainable for me, but fortunately it is already completely true for Petri.

Petri holds the fifteen minutes old baby right in his arms in the room next to the delivery room. When swaddled, the baby screams. From somewhere we hear the words of an exhausted woman, but Petri will never meet the woman who gave birth to our child.

It's wonderful to tell those closest to us that we have just had a little baby girl in St. Petersburg. We will only tell a few people the news, we would tell others only when little Tessa was safely in Finland.

With Tessa in his arms, Petri is happy that he had courage to leap in this adventure. Every day in the hospital is memorable with Tessa, but without language skills a bit challenging. It doesn't bother Petri as Tessa snuggles next to him contentedly. If they had an emergency, things would be taken care of. The entire staff is professional and, if necessary, you can get help in English by phone. You can call an interpreter, but often the translator app on your mobile phone is enough. The doctors show the baby's health information, but Petri doesn't understand a word of it. Doctors and nurses are at first a bit like Finnish tourists in Spain, who try to speak Finnish but when not understood speaking in Finnish again but louder this time rather than trying in English, and now louder with Russian. Petri translates the most important terms with Google. Fortunately, based on our previous visits, he had downloaded the Cyrillic alphabet to his phone.

Already on the second day after Tessa's birth, I must fly to St. Petersburg to visit just for a while. For the registration of the baby at the agency, which is required by Russian law, both of us must be physically present. Flying scares me after surgery and in the middle of radiation treatments, but there is no other option. Finnair's personnel are friendly, and the pilots are immediately informed of the situation. The medicines are ready and fortunately the flight goes well.

I'm going to the hospital by taxi. I see Tessa for the first time in the hospital corridor. She sleeps in Petri's arms with her cheek pressed against his shoulder. Petri carefully lifts the girl into my arms. You are finally real my dear child! Tessa's hat immediately gets wet from my tears. While I am here, Petri wouldn't get to hold the child anymore, I absorbed her warmth every passing moment.

In the evening, Tessa sleeps in a push-in baby bed on wheels. I quietly stroke the cheek of the sleeping little one. I can't even describe my feelings, so much love overwhelms me. We are finally there. Life is here. Our family is complete now. It would be necessary to bring the family together one way or another. I decide that we will spend Christmas together. If it doesn't work out otherwise, then I will come with the children to St. Petersburg to Tessa and Petri.

In the morning we would go to the office. After that, I would only have a few hours before returning to Finland for the next radiation treatment. At night I watch with Tessa and feed her the bottle milk brought by the nurses. I just want to watch this wonderful miracle, I'm so happy. I try to sleep for a while Tessa sleeps too, but mentally I'm in such an overactive state that nothing really comes of it.

A clinic representative will pick us up from the hospital. He speaks good English. I tell him that I'm afraid to leave Tessa in the hospital. I'm asking permission to take Tessa with me. He replies that Tessa is fine and that no one unrelated can get to Tessa. The nurses take good care of her. I'm scared, but I can't help but have faith. I want the matter to be dealt with quickly so that we can get back to our daughter.

The agency has a lot of couples taking care of different things. The friendly agency representative who processed our papers asks what Tessa's middle name Tuulikki means. The name Tessa is internationally known, but Tuulikki is not known in Russia. I can't think of any other explanation than that it's like a warm and fresh summer breeze. The clerk says that's a really good name and stamps our papers.

When we return to the hospital, Tessa is surrounded by doctors and nurses. I'm freaking out. Our contact person quickly clears up the situation and tells us that everything is fine. This is just a routine check. It's wonderful to have Tessa in my arms again. Hello little person, it's great that you came into our lives! We still make many trips together at home in Finland to the nearby forest. I try to remember every detail, every feeling and smell, which soon I won't be able to experience again other than from the pictures on my cell phone. I don't want to think about separating from Tessa yet. Petri calls the Finnish consulate in St. Petersburg to clarify Tessa's passport issue. I just hug the little ones and try to forget the world around us for a while. Tomorrow morning, I would already be in Finland strapped to a table at a radiotherapy clinic. After that, I would be in the district court, and who knows which all possible agencies to sort out Tessa's paperwork.

Tears fall from my cheeks into Tessa's hair as I hug her one more time. I look at Petri and he looks handsome and strong, but at the same time insecure and fragile. Above all, he seems unyielding when forced to do so. Petri once quoted Stephen Hawking to me: "No matter how difficult life seems, there is always something you can do and succeed in it. The most important thing is not to give up." Now it seems he was absolutely right. We have made the impossible a reality. My gaze lingers once more on our daughter squirming in the cradle before I take my bag and leave for the airport in the darkness of the morning.

After five days, Tessa and Petri will be able to move from the hospital to a hotel as planned, where the nurse will visit Tessa a few more times. Petri is happy, even though he is now alone with the baby without the help of nurses. Fortunately, Petri has experience with children, so everything goes well. His days are the same with formula feeding, sleeping and bathing. While Tessa sleeps, he reads a lot of e-books he has saved on his kindle.

We have decided from the beginning that someone will always monitor Tessa's breathing. We did the same with Topias, because he had reflux as a baby and was in danger of choking on vomit. We will immediately put the remote monitoring device into operation. Petri attaches a camera to Tessa's bed, which films Tessa. Thus, when Petri sleeps, one of us in Finland always watches over Tessa's sleep in turns. If necessary, we would wake up Petri by phone if something happened. Fortunately, nothing happens, everything goes well.

We have decided from the beginning that someone will always monitor Tessa's breathing. We did the same with Topias, because he had reflux as a baby and was in danger of choking on vomit. We will immediately put the remote monitoring device into operation. Petri attaches a camera to Tessa's bed, which films Tessa. Thus, when Petri sleeps, one of us in Finland always watches over Tessa's sleep in turns. If necessary, we would wake up Petri by phone if something happened. Fortunately, nothing happens, everything goes well.

The staff at the hotel are friendly and help Petri as much as possible. They told me afterwards that they were wondering where I had disappeared to and why Petri was taking care of the baby alone, but no one had dared to ask. Petri, on the other hand, is not kind of person to share personal things to people without them asking first.. So, everyone quickly fulfilled Petri's smallest requests. Petri goes back and forth with Tessa in the stroller in the hotel lobby. He sits in the lobby for coffee after Tessa falls asleep. The days are the same and there is no information about entering Finland. Petri decides to go see the sights of St. Petersburg with Tessa when the doctor gives permission to go outside with Tessa despite the slight frost. Petri pushes the tiny stroller forward in the slush. It's drizzling in St. Petersburg, visibility is really bad. The wind rustles in the walls of the apartment buildings in the narrow streets as if saying that Petri and the baby still have many cold journeys in these alleys ahead of them before they can order a taxi to take the irreplaceable beloved addition to the family to the train station towards Helsinki. St. Petersburg would be their home, maybe for a while or longer. As in Kenya, no one knows the length of time yet. However, the most important thing is that the child is already in your arms.

In the morning, the alarm rings early again so that we can reach the door of the district court again before eight. Would we get the necessary papers today to take Tessa home? The receptionists is telling me what additional information is still needed. There would again be visits to the consulate, the immigration office, visits to official translators for new documents to be translated and few visits on other places. I take water and my medicine and a piece of chocolate. I'm tired but there is no other choice but just keep moving forward. My father is waiting outside in the car. I guide him on how the day will go. First, I go to radiotherapy and then there is an office tour. The service at our local police station is friendly. Everyone lives with the spirit and hopes that different agencies will cooperate to help us get Tessa home.

The Immigration Office says that their unit that would handle our case is on the other side of Finland. No one can advise what reports and papers are required there. Irritated, I start a group call at the agency and include all the involved agencies and the consulate in St. Petersburg in the call. By negotiating together, it becomes clear what the different parties require from each other. I'll list a summary for everyone, what each needs to deliver and to whom. The joint plan is now clear. Then we try again to have the necessary documents for the judge together.

The weekend is approaching, and the streets are full of people doing Christmas shopping. Fortunately, there is still no information about the corona virus before Christmas 2019. The judge requires certain original documents from Russia, the digital delivery of them is not sufficient. What would we do now? Fortunately, our friendly contact person from the Finnish consulate in St. Petersburg is coming to Finland for a weekend vacation. He knows our difficult situation and promises to bring the documents to Finland in his way. My father takes me to meet him in Helsinki, and we get the papers in time for the next week.

Radiation treatments stress me so much that my hair falls out a lot and my health deteriorate. If only everything were okay in the district court today. However, the judge states that the Russian surrogacy law is still unclear to the district court in some respects. The judge wants the original, signed document from the lawyer on the relevant legal points, because otherwise the documents needed for the passport will not be issued. What on earth? How could it succeed in this situation? Petri would have to stay in St. Petersburg over Christmas. There is no other option but to go get the papers. I would have radiotherapy, but luckily the doctors and the radiotherapy clinic manage to arrange the matter so that the missed day is scheduled for the day after the last treatment in the calendar. My father's expression is stunned. He is no longer surprised by any turn of events when I tell him that in a couple of days, we will go to St. Petersburg instead of radiation treatment and in the morning we will fly back for radiation treatment the next day. Fortunately, the visa can be obtained quickly and soon I will be heading to Helsinki-Vantaa airport with my father.

The flight goes well again, and I open the phone in the taxi. Petri and Tessa would meet us in the hotel lobby. Petri has already been in contact with a lawyer, to whom we would go to meet immediately by taxi. We arrive at the hotel lobby and rush to our beloved baby. My father sees our daughter for the first time, and we are all teary eyed. We are so happy about Tessa. Still, the main thing is hurry. We need to get the necessary paper so that we have even a small hope of getting everything taken care of before Christmas. After that, a long Christmas break would begin over the turn of the year in both Russia and Finland, and the return would move somewhere in the distant future.

As we were about to leave the hotel door, the phone rang. I recognize the number of the District Court. On the phone is a judge handling our case, he has familiarized himself with Russian law during the night. He states that everything is exactly as we said, in order. There would be no need to travel to St. Petersburg. I will tell him laughing that we are already here. I request that he now email us the final signed paper as a scan. That way we can make sure everything is fine now. The document arrives quickly to my inbox, and I can see it on my smartphone.

Our joy knows no bounds. Finally, Tessa would get Finnish citizenship. I tell the whole story to the hotel staff, who rejoice with us and congratulate. We had visited a great Indian restaurant in the city centre in the summer. Instead of the planned office day, we head there for lunch. Oh, the feeling of relaxation that comes over me and my dad after everything. Petri too is relieved and happy to be able to spend a nice day together with us and, above all, that the situation is starting to resolve itself. Now we still need to get a passport for Tessa and she and Petri cross the border by train to Finland. In the middle of the treatments, I feel how joy and light are starting to return to our lives, as if my little girl is leading me out of the darkness.

I'll float to you
My own, my wanderer
I guide you to the chocolate shop and hide the evil from you
How do you know everything about me, even when you look at me for the
first time

One small life, big light inside
I look at the silent sleeper, I look at the bearer of comfort
I always keep close, I walk beside the road
For my escort is a newborn [19]

THE END

Over the boarder

I get a decision from the district court to confirm Petri's paternity. The document is needed at the Registration Office and the Immigration Office, which make the necessary decisions to enable Tessa's entry. Petri must wait in St. Petersburg for many more long days. The moment we've been waiting for is finally coming when everything will change. Petri sends Tessa's lovely passport photo from the photo studio to my cell phone, little Tessa. Smiling, I think it reminds me of the passport photo taken of Topias as a baby when we left for Germany. Petri is heading to the consulate with the papers, and we hope that he will make it to the train arriving in Helsinki that evening.

Everything goes well and Tessa gets her passport. Petri takes a deep breath of the cool December air as he walks out of the embassy. Now there would be no rush for anything. Tessa is finally ours and thanks to the passport she would soon be in Finland. They wouldn't have time for tonight's train, but there is room on the next evening's train and Petri buys tickets on the Internet. What a great gift: Tessa and Petri would come to Finland the night before my birthday. Petri walks calmly all the way from the embassy to the hotel. Christmas is coming and there are Christmas markets on the way, finally there is time to stop and look at them. At the hotel, Petri gives Tessa's passport to the reception. Officials have been asking for an explanation about the child's whereabouts every day for a couple of weeks. They admire the pink covers of the passport and assume that the colour is due to the gender of the child. To their disappointment, Petri explains that the colour of the passport refers to the deadline of the document and not to the gender of its holder. In the room, the stress of weeks is released. Petri sleeps almost the entire next day. When Tessa wakes up, Petri also wakes up, changes the diaper, feeds the girl and puts her back to sleep. At the same time, he falls asleep himself. December without snow is so dark that you lose track of time. At some point, Petri wakes up and thinks he missed the train. It's dark and it's a little past six in the morning. The train wouldn't leave until twelve hours later.

After a confused day, Petri and Tessa are finally at the Finlandski train station in St. Petersburg. Petri and Tessa squeeze into the train with all their belongings. Fortunately, Tessa falls asleep almost immediately when Petri has placed her in a car seat on the train bench.

The trip goes smoothly. After Vyborg, the Russian border officials board the train. Petri, who doesn't know Russian, tries to explain in English to border authorities who don't know English, based on documents in Russian, that the little child next to him is his and the mother waiting in Finland. The first border guard wonders about it for a while and then asks for help from another. In the end, both disappear somewhere with all the papers. Petri is anxiously waiting to see what happens next. After agonizing minutes, the first border officer comes back with the papers and hands them to Petri with a smile. He says something in Russian, which Petri interprets as meaning have a good trip. The Russian border officials leave, and the train now starts towards the Finnish border.

We were not completely sure of the attitude of the Finnish authorities towards surrogacy before the end of the surrogacy process. During the process, we have had to experience that, despite the warm thoughts of the authorities, moving things forward has not been easy. The attitude of the Finnish border authorities is exciting in advance, especially when you remember the commotion at the border when Melissa came to Finland. My parents and I are anxiously waiting for information about when the Russian-Finnish border has been crossed.

Petri is sitting next to a wheezing Tessa when the border guard gets on the train. Petri hands his passport and Tessa the passport made the day before at the embassy. The border guard checks the information on the pink passport and smilingly looks at the baby who is sniffing in his sleep: - Oh, she's brand new. He hands the passports back to Petri and continues his journey.

We get a message from Petri that the boarder has been crossed! He and Tessa are in Finland. There is no limit to our joy. We leave for the Helsinki railway station. It's the night before my birthday, a little before Christmas. I could not wish for a better birthday than spending it together with our four children.

We drive the car in front of my workplace to the parking lot, which is located right next to the train station. I gratefully look at the windows of my workplace and think of my managers and co-workers, current and former. The support of all of them has been invaluable in this long journey we have travelled to our children.

Now I finally feel that I will soon be able to lift the noose from my neck. We're almost there. All the evil starts to drain away from me, and fear is left behind as a black pond for street paving. In this moment, everything changes. I'm finally getting my wings back. Even though my strength is low, my grip is strong. I walk with my father towards the railway tracks, it's getting close to midnight. It's quiet and there aren't many people around. We are waiting. In the distance we see the lights of a train slowly approaching the station. There you are, dear ones, our little baby and Petri. After a few minutes, the train stops next to the platform. I look through the windows of the train, looking for familiar faces. I see Petri in the hallway walking towards the door with a safety cradle in his hand while pulling suitcases. I rush to receive the baby. I wrap my arms around my child so gently that I would not only hurt him but at the same time so strongly that nothing could separate us anymore. I grab the seat belt of the baby seat and make sure you are safe. Little one. Happiness and joy. I hold out my hand and you take my finger gently. I will never let go. We are finally there.

At home, all the siblings stay up at night and wait for the little sister. It's the most moving moment in the world when the siblings come to see who's smiling inside the covers. She is happy Tessa. Our joy!

Tessa is finally home, and all is well. I wake up at night to see if she's okay. I can feel the cruel female character trying to shake us once more. I peek through the blinds into the yard. I can already see her further away, just a blur. You no longer get to control us and shake our happiness. We're finally trying to be happy, now it's our turn. I remember my friend saying on our walk that since I myself have created a dark figure in my mind, I can also destroy it myself. That's what I am going do. The dark figure would no longer come to mock of our troubles.

While taking care of Tessa at night, I suddenly notice a birthmark on her. Great is my astonishment, for it is in the shape of a four-leaf clover! Now our four-leaf clover is complete.

All our children are super happy of Tessa and each of them quickly develops their own special relationship with her. Together, they play with Tessa and tell each other about the day's events when one of them has been involved in hobbies. The joy is back. Teenagers don't have to be so big anymore, they can return to childhood games and memories with Tessa. After the difficulties, our family is stronger together than ever before. This happiness is worth all the hardships I have experienced:

I thank you for the tears,
late nights
happiness is moments
when you make us perfect
You are beautiful
fragile and innocent
you are ours
and I'm yours
as long as I can [20]

Pandemic. Information about the spread of the coronavirus takes over the news. Fortunately, Petri and Tessa were able to cross the border home to Finland just before the pandemic. Half a year after their return home, we read in the news that due to travel restrictions caused by the corona virus, more than fifty babies born by surrogates are waiting for their parents in Ukraine. We are happy that Petri and Tessa made it to Finland before the corona epidemic, but at the same time we feel great sympathy for the parents who cannot get to their babies because of the corona.

Organizing the christening of Tessa will be delayed until next autumn due to corona restrictions. In the same autumn, the elder brother Topias' holy communion is celebrated. We keep them in close to our Home, where Matias is also buried. I look out the window at the communion and see the cemetery. It feels like Matias is present at our family party. We got to keep him with us for a while. We had four children and one angel child with memories. If you count all the miscarriages, we had many angel children. Brave we faced it all. Our experiences with all their emotions bound us together as a family.

If you look at us from the outside and don't know everything that happened, everything can seem like a dream come true. That's what it is for us. We got everything we hoped for, but we had to work hard for it. Our family has not been basking in the pages of interior design magazines. We have always taken care of the children's needs, and they have had fun experiences. Children's joy has always been the most important thing. At the same time, in our house, the mouldings have been in a state of disrepair and clothes are drying unfashionably here and there. Everything didn't have to be "just right". I experienced the same when I was little in my childhood home, when we slept happily in sleeping bags in the living room in the middle of a construction site. It's not that I don't care about the condition of our home. I just haven't really had time and been able to renovate before all the kids and Tessa were home. The best thing is a normal everyday life without tension and drama. That's what we strive for, but of course you can't influence everything.

When our family is finally together, my next goal is to recover from the surgery and get back to work. As my return-to-work approaches, Finland is still living through the corona season. I don't need to do hair, make-up or be presentable every day when working from home. Fortunately, time is saved because I am still extremely tired from everything we experienced. The final goal is to get a normal life back after almost twenty years. I start the rehabilitation lightly by pushing Tessa outside in the pram for bit longer day by day.

Spending all the days with Tessa, I get to look closely at her and start to wonder about the strange looking blood vessel between her eyes. I will discuss the matter at the consultation, where we will be referred to eye surgery. Again, I find myself afraid of something bad happening. During the past weeks, I had time to think a lot. I realize in the midst of fear, while taking care of the happy Tessa that no one can take away these moments that I have been able to spend with Tessa and all my children. These moments remain in my heart now that I'm busy with Tessa. Even a short moment with her at hospital in Russia will not disappear from my memories, no matter what happens. I won't lose the good times spent with all our children over the years, even if something bad happens. Those moments remain in my memories. I try to photograph our moments together so that I can always return to them together with the children. I turn the pictures into wall calendars. I can't control what happens next, I can only try to handle things now as best as I can. I don't have to wake up at night to monitor the children's breathing and call the older children in distress. I have to trust that everything will work out as it is meant to.

Fortunately, the painful wait of a few weeks turns into joy. According to Tessa's eye examinations, everything is fine. I also start taking care of my own sleep and well-being so that I can be a mother to my children. I can't change yesterday, I don't know tomorrow's events, it's just this now, this moment. I try to live it as well as I can and give good memories to my children and make the right choices for tomorrow. I have banished the dark figure once and for all. Fear no longer defines my life.

Good, thank you

It's the school Christmas party. For a long time, I haven't been going to different parties at school because it hurt me a lot to see babies being born to families. Now I encourage my mind and Tessa and I go to the primary school Christmas party. After radiation treatments, I only have a thin layer of hair on my head, but that's okay. I lift the few hair strands I have into a ponytail and throw something from the wardrobe over me that will fit on me after the swelling caused by radiation treatments. The children and the children's friends are happy to see Tessa at the party. We try to be sensitive so that someone who may be grieving the loss of their own baby does not suffer from us.

After Christmas, a year later, I have a follow-up MRI. I am scared when I go to the MRI scan, but luckily my head is clear. The illness still leaves a shadow, but on the other hand, I can enjoy every moment more than before. I prioritize everything in life drastically. I decide what is important, I think about what makes me happy and what is mandatory. Maybe the illness, even in its brutality, was necessary for me to properly understand the values of life and the limits of my own endurance.

The first agency visit with Tessa in Finland is handled well. The Population Register Center still wants to see Tessa "live" before the papers are made official. We also visit the local police station where all the officers come to congratulate us. They had wondered how we were doing and whether we would finally have a child. At the pharmacy, I unexpectedly meet my old colleague, whose son he adopted from Thailand was our bright spot in our fight against infertility. It is gratifying to exchange information. I am also grateful to the doctor who encouraged us to have a surrogate birth, even though he was not able to help us concretely due to obstacles in Finnish law. Circle closes.

A new morning. Tessa wakes up with a D-shaped mouth. I take her in my arms. Tessa wants to hold my big nose many times for a long time. I realize that what I was bullied for at school is now everything. I still can't help but check on Tessa when I wake up at night from a nightmare, heat or whatever. Now, however, the alarmed "Is Tessa breathing?" thought is quickly turning into another. I want to look at her, my lovely child. It's so amazing that she in here and so cute when she sleeps. I have the same idea about all my children, and I have gone through the same process with each of them. Now it's just that my whole nightmare is finally over and I'm getting on with the normal everyday life worries of a parent. I love everyday life and doing ordinary things. I can focus on everything better when the constant worry is gone, the worry of losing my children and my own health. I'm finally more than just getting there, I have arrived and I'm safe. Maybe not forever, but at least right now. I want to enjoy this moment and save it in my mind and maybe take a photo of it as a treasure for myself in case of a bad day.

A person changes during his life. If the couple's shared wishes and goals do not grow in the same direction with the spouses, the relationship can run into a wall, whether we are traveling by car or canoeing on the river. We have managed to survive together until now. Maybe soon I will dare to trust that the fourth, happy phase in my life will begin.

Our family is together now. Both us parents and children feel like we have gained mental peace after all these years. Gugu says while writing this book that even though so much has happened in our family, it's pretty great that we're all alive. Melissa, on the other hand, states that, despite everything, whenever we are asked "how are you", we always answer, 'Good, thank you'. It's a standard, easy way to answer. When asked about the events of the weekend, I say that these days we do a little bit of everything. I can't begin to explain the whole story, because so much is still happening to us all the time.

The kids are right. A lot has happened and is still happening. The most important thing is this moment and the fact that we are together. The children founded a club called Team Nuora when they were small. All children in the family are included in the club. They strive to share that common good in other situations in their lives, even outside the home. No one would be left alone. Our children see the world as one and everyone is equal.

The most important lesson to share from my journey is that you should never stop trying and give up if your dream or goal is important to you and it promotes or at least does not undermine the well-being of the earth. No matter how big or small your dream is, you can succeed on it if you dare to start the journey to achieve it. It requires the ability to take risks. Planning, flexibility, quickness, positivity, searching for a new path, asking for help and giving help will get you there. Few survive here alone. Together we can achieve a lot. My father has said he wouldn't change a day of his life. I would not change a single choice I made.

Trust and hope that you can get through everything. Whatever happened, you will survive. In the end, the time will turn all your memories to comfort, and you'll find a way to get stronger and move on. There is still a lot of good things to see and experience in front of you, if only you observed your surroundings with the same precision as Topias on the floor of the safari car when examining special ants.

It is a warm day in May and the apple trees in our yard are blooming. Children's laughter fills the yard. Melissa is sitting next to me on the steps of the terrace and thoughtfully pondering the many purposes of lives. She has come to conclusion that the ultimate purpose of life is to live. I smile at the young person's well-articulated thought. We focus on life with every cell in us. I'm not asking for anything anymore. I got everything from life.

218

EPILOGUE

When I finish the book in 2021, the Ministry of Justice of Finland will investigate whether to allow non-commercial surrogacy in situations defined separately in the legislation. We are following the progress of the matter with interest. We hope it will be helpful for those who have a loved one who can help by offering their uterus. Hopefully, the legislation would also take into account those who do not have a close relative who could act as a surrogate. On our own trip, we experienced first-hand that since there is no legislation on surrogacy, the authorities could not give us any advice or support in advance. In Finland, the authorities can only act within the framework of the law. After our child was born, the authorities had the means to act in the way defined by the law, in which case everyone was helpful to us and told us how the process would proceed from now on and seemed to be happy for us.

We took this path because we had no choice. For the sake of the child, one will find strength to fight. At the end, our feelings are relief and bottomless gratitude. We feel that our hearts are full of happiness for our four children, and we remember the fifth and others who passed away with warmth.

Now, while I'm writing the book in the middle of the pandemic, we've been at home and alternated with Petri on care leave. At the same time, the other has been working remotely from home, which has contributed to our family becoming even closer. We can breathe a sigh of relief that the trip to St. Petersburg and the whole process were completed before the restrictions on the borders. We were very lucky. Now, a couple of years later, the borders are practically closed again, this time due to international sanctions imposed due to the war of aggression started by Russia. Newspapers once again tell about newborns waiting for their parents in Kiev, who the parents cannot pick up. This time the reason is rocket attacks and bombings. Foreign surrogacy has become uncertain. Adoption queues are getting longer and international adoption to Finland is only possible from a handful of countries. We feel deep sympathy for all couples and families who are waiting for a child from somewhere.

Forensic dentist Helena Ranta stated in the Plan International newsletter: "More important than what we remember is what we must not forget." 21 When I read that, I thought of all the children I met in Africa and China who hoped that they would find a loving family. I also remember the parents I meet everywhere, who from the bottom of their hearts hope to bring their own child home. Alive.

In Finland, the culture at our workplaces has changed during our long journey so that today it is allowed or even encouraged to open up more about ourselves. On the other hand, with life experience, you yourself dare to open your thoughts and feelings to others more.

There are several levels in life, such as how I appear to loved ones, how to the neighbourhood and how at work. In the end, we decided to tell about everything we experienced. Now I can be myself in every place and situation.

Believe in your dreams and pursue them without giving up, look for new routes to get there. What happens doesn't define you unless you decide so for yourself.

I would like every child to know that they are valuable:

Where were you made?
Beyond the stars
Moulded with care

Please don't ever
Lose that look

What else can you carry?
High like that you sing
Nothing that heavy can come
That it would crush you

Beautiful little person
You are unique
Whatever comes up
Another like you, never will again [22]

222

THANK YOU

I am grateful for this journey to so many. Thank you, Petri, for taking the time to walk this journey of years with me. Thank you for your love and for not giving up even in tight spots. My children, the greatest gifts of my life, thank you for every day and the most important events in my life. Your joy is my light. My parents, no words are enough to express my gratitude to you for your sincere help and unconditional understanding in every situation. Thank you, to our family, relatives, friends, acquaintances and even strangers, for example in hospital waiting rooms, from whom we have received support, hugs and empathetic looks in joy and sadness, as well as encouraging words, wonderful messages, help in everyday life. Everything that has moved us forward in our fight. Thank you, our children's teachers, who have genuinely cared about our children and been flexible in the storms of our lives. Many thanks to all our employers who have supported us over the years and made all this possible. Thank you to the managers who empathetically understood us in every situation and the great colleagues who ran to help whenever life pulled the rug from under our feet. Thank you doctors, nurses and other professionals from different fields who helped us and experts from organizations, who did not give up even when all the stones had already been turned over. There is always a chance to get there if we just don't give up. Even if through a thousand twists and turns.

Thank you to those of you who helped in the various stages of the creation of this book. Your help and wise words have been invaluable.

Thank you, Tanja for all the hard work and inspiring comments in making this English version of my story happen. It would not have been possible without your enthusiasm.

And finally, thank you dear reader for taking the time to join me on this journey.

REFERENCE

1 Translated from Finnish poem: Mika Lehto: Virga (2019)

2 Translated from Finnish poem: Aino Suhola's production

3 Translated from Finnish poem: Tommy Tabermannin poem: Positiivarit-website: https://www.positiivarit.fi/

4 Translated from Finnish poem: Tommy Tabermann: Intohimon panttivanki (1980)

5 The Office. NBC Universal Television Distribution (2005-2013)

6 Translated from Finnish poem Värssyt.fi-website: https://varssyja.wordpress.com/vauva-aiheisia-runoja/

7 Translated from Finnish poem: Anne-Mari Kaskinen: https://www.positiivarit.fi/varssypankki/aiti/jos-on-kerran-aidiksi-syntynyt/

8 Translated from Finnish song: Pave Maijanen: Pidä huolta. Kaikki nämä vuodet –album (1992) Songwriter: Pave Maijanen

9 Translated from Finnish poem: A.A. Milne: Winnie the Pooh- poem: Sitaatit.fi

10 Translated from Finnish: Chinese pro verb: https://fi.pinterest.com/pin/490188740669002436/

11 Translated from Finnish: Chinese pro verb: https://www.special-dictionary.com/proverbs/keywords/diamond/

12 Translated from Finnish song: Robin Packalen: Sua varten. Suuren ikäluokan lapsi –album (2014) Songwriters: Jimi Constantine / Jonas Olsson / Tobias Granbacka

13 Translated from Finnish song: Kurt Westerlund: Sä jäät mun uniin. Sä jäät mun uniin –album (2020) Songwriter: Kurt Westerlund

14 Translated from Finnish song: Jannika B: Aplodit mulle. Toinen nainen –album (2019) Songwriter: Jannika Wirtanen

15 Translated from Finnish song: Jannika B: Itseni herra. Šiva – album (2014) Songwriter: Heidi Maria Paalanen / Jannika Wirtanen

16 Translated from Finnish song: Vesala: Uusia unelmia –single (2019) Songwriters: Joonas Angeria / Paula Julia Vesala

17 Translated from Finnish song: Johanna Kurkela: Sun särkyä anna mä en. Marmoritaivas-album (2007) Songwriters: Tomi Aholainen / Heikki Karkelae

18 Translated from Finnish song: Mariska: 11. Vain elämää –season (2020) Banijay Finland –production.

19 Translated from Finnish song: Useita esittäjiä: Lohtu. Live Aid Uusi Lastensairaala (2017) Songwriters: Tuure Kilpeläinen, Saima Vilhelmiina Hyökki

20 Translated from Finnish song: Suvi Teräsniska: Sinä olet kaunis (2016) Songwriter: Petri Somer

21 Forensic dentist, Plan International honorary chairman Helena Ranta: Planin newsletter (2021)

22 Translated from Finnish song: Johanna Kurkela: Ainutlaatuinen. Hyvästi, Dolores Haze –album (2010) Markus Koskinen / Teemu Brunila

CPSIA information can be obtained
at www.ICGtesting.com
Printed in the USA
LVHW051655271222
735836LV00008B/846